Iran's
Secret Pogrom

GEOFFREY NASH

Iran's
Secret Pogrom

*The Conspiracy to Wipe Out
the Baha'is*

SUFFOLK

NEVILLE SPEARMAN

First published in Great Britain in 1982 by
Neville Spearman Limited
The Priory Gate, Friars Street, Sudbury, Suffolk

ISBN 0 85435 005 5 (hardcover)
ISBN 0 85435 015 2 (paperback)

Typeset in 11/13pt Baskerville by
MS Typesetting, Castle Camps, Cambridge
Printed and bound in Great Britain by
Biddles Ltd, Guildford and King's Lynn

CONTENTS

PREFACE

Today, Iran is in turmoil. Nearly three years after a bloody revolution, the bodies go on accumulating, and anxiety and bewilderment about the country's future must even now be gripping the majority of her people. Earthquakes have added to the total of the dead, and deepened the consternation of Iranians. The suffering has been widely distributed among the ranks of this once proud nation. But among those who look apprehensively towards an uncertain future, there is one section of the population in particular that has cause for dread.

At the time of writing (November 1981) there is great trepidation and fear for the lives of the Baha'i community of Iran, estimated at between 300,000 and 400,000 people, and represented throughout the extent of the country. The world's press has reported the plight of this community extensively, and television and radio broadcasts have already given many hours of reportage and analysis of the situation. National and international Parliaments have passed resolutions calling upon Iran to respect the human rights of this minority, unacknowledged in the new Islamic Constitution and derisively referred to as a political sect by the authorities in Tehran. The United Nations has lifted up its voice in the form of a declaration by a subcommittee of its Human Rights Commission. Yet still the position of the Baha'is in Iran grows worse almost daily. It seems even realistic to speak, as the author of a report in the *Sunday Times* on 20 September 1981, of 'a final solution', in which the third of a million Baha'is suffer a holocaust similar to that of the Jews at the hands of Nazi Germany.

This book has been written in order that the truth about

1 The destruction of a holy place: The House of the Bab in Shiraz — razed to the ground, September 1979, Graffiti reads 'Bahaism is the Fifth Column in Iran — therefore it should be annihilated'.

2 The demolition in progress.

the Baha'is in Iran be told. Their story must not become tragedy; the human race otherwise will have again the blood of many thousands of innocent people on its hands, simply because their religious creed aroused the hatred of the State in which they dwelt, and the rest of mankind did nothing to prevent their deaths.

INTRODUCTION

Professor Manuchihr Hakim, a renowned researcher in the field of anatomy, was in his clinic as usual on 12 January, 1981. This Iranian physician, celebrated for his discoveries in gastroenterology (for which he was twice cited in the prestigious French medical encyclopedia, *Le Rouvière*) and widely known as the author of numerous text books and treatises, had returned to Tehran not long before from visiting Europe.

His friends abroad had advised him not to go back, for not only was this a time of great tension in war-torn, revolutionary Iran, but Professor Hakim himself had good reason to fear for his personal safety. He replied to their anxious warnings that he had a duty to the people in need whom he had served in his capacities as director of a Tehran hospital, founder of a Home for the Aged, and unofficial peacemaker between the different racial, religious, and social backgrounds in Iran. He might have added to these distinctions, the *Legion d'honneur* he had received from the French Government for his humanitarian services.

It was his duty to return to Iran, and this explained his presence in his clinic. It was a Monday; that past weekend he had received anonymous threats to his life. Not long before that he had experienced a lengthy interrogation by the revolutionary guards, during which he had withstood coercion to reveal a list of physicians in which they were particularly interested.

As he closed his clinic, after seeing his last patient, unidentified gunmen broke into the premises, and shot Professor Hakim dead. The authorities made no effort to identify or bring to justice his assassins. Instead the local revolutionary court responded by summarily confiscating all of the victim's property.

Six months later, on the B.B.C. television programme, *Newsnight*, (July 7) Professor Hakim's son, Paul, identified the reason for his father's execution in the fact that he was a Baha'i. The list of doctors the revolutionary guards had wanted from Professor Hakim had been a list of specifically Baha'i doctors. Professor Hakim was a noted Baha'i — he had served on the national governing body of the Baha'is of Iran ('National Spiritual Assembly') for over twenty-five years, several times holding the position of chairman. The old peoples' home he had founded had been entitled, the 'Baha'i Home for the Aged'; he had been a director at the Baha'i Hospital in Tehran, where patients from all religious backgrounds were treated. The threats against Professor Hakim's life, which were repeated, were without doubt from fanatical people objecting to the fact that he was a Baha'i. Professor Hakim had been fully aware of all this himself when he returned to Iran. He would have known that his eminent position in the Baha'i community of Iran laid him open to the kind of attention other prominent Baha'is had already received. The executions of Baha'is by firing squads in Tehran, Tabriz and Yazd; the arrest and disappearance of his old colleagues on the National Spiritual Assembly of the Baha'is of Iran — he would have been quite aware of these facts.

Another doctor, Faramarz Samandari, would also have recognized the danger he faced in remaining in Iran as he sent his Canadian wife, Anita, and his three children to safety in Canada, at the outbreak of the Iranian Revolution, on January 16, 1979. His wife subsequently recounted: 'I think this was the turning point for us. By this time most of the foreigners had left through air-lifts; Sam and his colleagues urged me to go and take the children to safety ... People have asked me why he also did not flee ... He had a strong sense of duty and felt he could not leave his parents and such courageous friends alone at this time'. Her account continues:

On April 21, 1980, Dr. Samandari was arrested by the Islamic government and imprisoned in Tabriz. He was charged with "running the Baha'i centers in Tabriz", working for SAVAK . . . and spreading prostitution.

These unjust accusations are always levelled at Baha'is.

. . .

Despite these trumped up charges Faramarz had no trial, just several hearings where he was encouraged to renounce his faith. He steadfastly refused.

The days in prison were long and tedious for a man used to being very active. Sometimes he was called to the prison infirmary to treat prisoners. Once a week a close relative was allowed to visit for a short while. Always there was the hope that soon this madness would end.

Then on July 14, late at night and in the cover of darkness, he was informed he would die; so he composed a brief will, prayed, and prepared himself. On hearing the decision many prisoners and guards wept.

At midnight he and a dear friend were executed in the streets of Tabriz. As they were led to their death several unfortunate others who had been convicted of drug peddling, etc., shouted, "We are guilty, but why kill the kind doctor?"

Nuk is a small village near Birjand in Khurasan. On 22 November, 1980, an elderly couple returned home from their day's work on the farm. At 10.00 p.m., Muhammad-Husayn Ma'sumi went out in the moonlight to fill the animals' feeding trough. When her husband did not return, the old lady called out. Suddenly several masked men entered the room, and without speaking they grabbed her and tied her with rope. They took her into a corner, and covered her with a heavy wooden door brought from elsewhere on the farm. When they put some dry wood on top of the door, soaked it in kerosene, and then poured the liquid over her clothes, she realised the errand they had come on. She told her neighbours after the attack: 'They set me on fire with matches and a lighter and stood for a few minutes to make sure the flames were high enough to reduce me to ashes in a short time'. Then she knew what had happened to her husband: his charred remains were found in a nearby ditch by neighbours, raised by the sound of the old man's cries. The old lady lived to see her dead husband's remains in the place where he had been murdered; she herself was probably struck on the head by her assailants who were still hiding in the vicinity, for when the neighbours returned to her she was speechless. She returned to her house and was found there shut up alone several day's later by her son-in-law. On reaching hospital she lapsed into a coma and died six days later. On 28 December, the *Observer* reported:

> In a village in eastern Iran last month, a man and his wife, members of the Bahai faith, were dragged from bed by masked men in the middle of the night, taken outside, doused in paraffin and burnt alive.

On 8 September, 1980, an announcement made on Radio Yazd in the morning said that in order to compensate for the loss of Muslim believers killed during the revolutionary disturbances the previous year, seven Baha'i spies had been executed. The news was repeated in several bulletins, and a videotape of the trial of the executed was shown on television two days later. The prosecution read the charges and one of the prisoners arose to give the statement of the defence, which was distorted and muffled by the television engineers. In his congregational prayers the next day, an Ayatollah of Yazd, preaching against the executed, invited the faithful to append their signatures to a petition approving of the action of the revolutionary courts in sentencing the Baha'is to death. A few hundred heeded his request, and next day the media reported that thousands of people had signed in approval of the court's verdict.

Of the seven who died in Yazd, several were members of the Local Spiritual Assembly of the Baha'is of Yazd. Others were active in other capacities in the teaching and administration of their Faith. The oldest was one 'Abdu'l-Vahhab, whose age was estimated as between eighty-five and ninety. He had a pronounced stoop which prevented him from standing erect, so that his body showed three bullet wounds in his abdomen, and another in his chest. It was also clear that he had been shot through the forehead.

A few months earlier, in June 1980, Yusuf Subhani was shot in the Evin prison in Tehran. A fellow Baha'i who was present at the prison with the condemned man's relatives, reports the following details about the man's death:

> Our meeting with Mr. Subhani lasted for 45 minutes, and in an atmosphere of enthusiasm, joy, and heroism . . . addressing his family he admonished them to avoid having any sense of revenge against those who had given false testimony at his trial, as he had left them to God, who would surely punish the wrongdoers.
>
> With great respect one of the guardsmen said that the time of the visit was over. Mr. Subhani embraced his family and relatives and later embraced all of the guardsmen who were waiting, kissed them, and told them how grateful he was to them. At the end he embraced and kissed Hah-Aqa Salihi (commander of the firing squad).
>
> When he shook hands and embraced me at the last moment, he jokingly said, 'They are going to kill *me*! Why are *your* hands so cold? See how warm mine are!'
>
> He returned to his cell with the same firm steps and erect posture. All of the guards accompanying him, as well as those stationed in the area who were having dinner, were astonished at him.

During that same summer, the anxiety of the Baha'is in Iran was greatly increased by the following series of events:

21 August 1980.
Eleven Baha'is were summarily arrested during the course of a meeting in a private home in Tehran. All of them were well-known Baha'is and nine of them composed the entire membership of the National Spiritual Assembly of the Baha'is of Iran (NSA). Their names are as follows:

Manuhir Qa'im-Maqami
Husayn Naji
Yusif Qadimi
Ibrahim Rahmani
Hushang Mahmudi

'Abdu'l-Husayn Taslimi
'Ata'u'llah Muqarrabi
Mrs. Bahiyyih Nadiri
Kambiz Sadiqzadih
Dr. Abbasiyan
Hishmat'u'llah Rawhani

These eleven Baha'is disappeared between 4 – 6 p.m. local time. An armed group appeared at the house apparently with a written order for their arrest. (Subsequently, their status has officially been changed to 'disappeared' persons.)

24 August.
All efforts to locate the prisoners were frustrated. Misleading and contradictory statements as to their whereabouts were given by officials. It was ascertained that the Attorney-General, Ayatollah Quddusi had given the order for the arrest of the eleven Baha'is, but the person entrusted with carrying it out denied all knowledge of the affair.

28 August.
The wives of some of the prisoners met with Ayatollah Beheshti and presented a petition to him. He undertook to enquire into the matter but subsequently reported that his investigations were inconclusive.

(It was discovered that at least some of the Baha'is were being held at the Evin prison in Tehran. However, the authorities refused to confirm this. Relatives and fellow Baha'is contacted the Speaker of the Majlis, Mr. Rafsanjani, who told them the eleven had been arrested for involvement in the recent attempt at a coup d'etat.)

18 September.
The Attorney-General stated that eleven Baha'is had been arrested because of their participation in a recent abortive coup.

9 October.
The wife of one of the missing Baha'is saw Mr. Rafsanjani

who informed her that the eleven had not been arrested by the government, and asked her where they were.

(Two more Baha'is, one of them the owner of the house where the eleven had met, were taken into custody, and questioned as to the eleven's whereabouts.)

12 October.
Mr. Rafsanjani informed wives of two of the missing Baha'is that they had been illegally arrested, and therefore should have resisted arrest. The wives replied that the court order for the arrests had been produced, but Rafsanjani persisted in his opinion that the Baha'is should have resisted arrest.

(The Attorney-General in another interview with the wives of the missing Baha'is, said he had not ordered their arrest, and admitted his responsibility to find out their whereabouts. He phoned the Evin prison in their presence, but the prison denied having any Baha'i prisoners.)

3 November.
After 70 days there was still no reliable information as to the whereabouts of the eleven Baha'is. No documents could be found affirming government orders for the arrest of the eleven missing Baha'is.   *Adapted from an official Baha'i account.*

Subsequent reports suggest that the eleven are not in the Evin prison, and so their whereabouts are now unknown. Like three other well-known Baha'is in Tehran, they had been kidnapped because of their prominence in the Baha'i Faith. Their kidnappers must have presumed that their loss would leave the Baha'i Community leaderless. Indeed, the majority of Baha'is murdered, executed or kidnapped in Iran since the Islamic Revolution have been prominent in the administration of their religion.

A new, ominous development in the story of persecution against members of the Baha'i Faith in Iran since 1979 was the execution of two Baha'is in Shiraz, not only under the charge of political involvement under the Shah, supporting SAVAK, and aiding prostitution, but actually for being members of Baha'i institutions. Hitherto, all persecutions had been denied by the authorities on the grounds that the accused had been convicted under the above charges, and not because of their religion. The Shiraz executions occurred on 17 March 1981, and inaugurated a new spate of executions of Baha'is for that year.

On 14 June, seven members of the Baha'i local assembly in Hamadan were executed. On 23 June, seven well-known Baha'is in Tehran met the same fate; and again in Tabriz, nine Baha'is died at the hands of the executioner in July, to add to the two who had died the previous year in Tabriz (includding Dr. Samandari).

Two of those who died in Hamadan were doctors of medicine, increasing the rôle-call of Baha'i doctors executed or murdered for their religion. Three were brothers-in-law; the ages of the dead ranged from 38 to 60. But the worst thing was that they had been tortured. The Baha'is have released the following details:

Muhammad Baqir Habibi — his shoulder had been broken and smashed

Dr. Nasir Vafa'i — his thighs had been cut open and he was shot twice

Dr. Firooz Na'imi — his back had been broken and he was shot seven times

Husayn Mutlaq-Arani — not tortured but had been shot nine times

Husayn Khandil — the fingers of one hand pressed and smashed, and his back was burned

Muhammad Habibi — his back was burned and he was shot five times

Taraz'ullah Khuzayn — his chest and left hand were smashed and he was shot seven times

Whether, or how, these outrageous contraventions of human rights will end is at present as uncertain as the storm-tossed future of Iran itself. One thing is sure: the history of the Baha'i religion in Iran has been thus far a tale of great suffering and loss — it is a past that can be charted by the persecutions and pogroms unleashed against the followers of a young religion who early on gave up their right to fight back with weapons, and whose descendants now face the same dilemma as did their forefathers: renounce your religion, or lay down your life . . .

CHAPTER ONE

The reasons why . . .
Origins of the persecution of the Baha'i Community to 1955

What is the reason behind the persecution of these people from such different walks of life? We have seen that their crime was, in the eyes of their assassins, that they were Baha'is; in fact they have their place in a role-call that stretches into tens of thousands, and goes back nearly a century and a half. For this persecution of Baha'is in Iran is no new thing — on the contrary, it is a stain on Iranian history that, obscure as it may be to the outer world, is of great significance to any view of the pattern of Iranian society.

The West is intrigued, perplexed, outraged by the events and upheavals it has witnessed going forward in Iran in the last few years. It supported the regime of the Shah of Iran without in the least understanding the culture or psychology of the society over which he ruled; it remains completely estranged from the complexities that have resulted from his downfall.

Western technology supported the regime of the Shah, and in return the Western countries obtained oil, and in later years, investment in Western economies of the Iranian oil wealth. Iranians came to live in the smart areas of Paris, London, Los Angeles and New York. They appeared to be rich, eager to adopt Western luxuriousness, and ready to indulge themselves in all the frivolities El Dorado had to offer — very often, these oil-rich Iranians displayed all the vulgarity of *arrivistes*.

Within the Shah's Iran itself, the disparity between, on the one hand, the international set, the real-estate owners, and the financiers, the new elite with their American degrees and large salaries — and on the other, the urban proletariat, barely arrived from the neglected country and agricultural areas, ignorant, still under the sway of traditional Iranian Islamic values, created a two-nations society. But the social polarisation of Iran was even more complicated by the political system of the country. The Shah's regime was an absolutist one, as the world now is aware — it denied political expression even to the rich merchant class, how much less the working class of South Tehran. When the revolution, which we can now see was inevitable, united all sections of Iranian society and toppled the Shah, it was also inevitable that it should draw its ideology from the most powerful anti-Western, anti-capitalist force in Iran; not Marxism, for political consciousness was rudimentary, but Shi'ite Islam.

Shi'ite Islam, the minority branch of the great religious schism that divided Islam from its early years, remains a largely reactionary force in Iran. In the previous century, the Shi'ite clerics supported the Qajar dynasty, and helped form the corrupt and venal character of the country, now greatly declined from its former glory. These clerics divided over the constitutional movement, but even those who supported reform did so largely in the hope of securing an Islamic state over which they themselves would preside. The clergy as a whole have remained rooted in outlook to an ideology formed centuries before, over which the sole custodians are themselves.

The twentieth century revolutions that swept Iran in the name of constitutionalism and reform left the Shi'ite clergy behind. With the downfall of the last Qajar Shah in 1925, their fate was sealed. The new Pahlavi dynasty founded by Reza Shah was a secular power — the clergy, though not as drastically as in Kemal Ataturk's secular Turkey, were stripped of their privileges and power. They lost their outward trappings of distinction too — people no longer came to them with gifts and pleas, nor kissed their hands and robes, nor heeded their strictures.

But though the clergy were in decline, the influence of

Shi'ite belief was ingrained in the Iranian people, and was linked with patriotism and memories of past glory. The Pahlavi rulers were intent on creating a different kind of mystique from the past — from pre-Islamic Persia, before her ancient language and religion were replaced by the civilization of Islam, and when her kings were feared by half of the world. Muslim culture, no longer espoused by the state, sought a political influence and found it, as the mosque and seminary became centres of opposition to the secular regime.

The opulence and inequalities of the new Iran angered the poor and the traditionalist. With justification they loathed the importation of Western technology, the hunger for money and ostentation amongst the minority of the prosperous. The clergy were able to capitalise on the alienation of the Iranian masses and won back — how temporarily time will tell — an influence over them. In return, they strengthened the xenophobia of the ignorant, did nothing to temper the superstition of the uneducated, and inculcated a hatred of all things Western — including Marxism.

It is here that the Baha'is enter. The enmity of the Shi'ite clergy towards the Baha'is is, and always had been, completely implacable. Its basis lies in religion, but it derives a great deal of its vehemence from the fear of the clergy that the Baha'is might one day supplant them.

The Baha'i Faith developed out of a messianic early nineteenth-century movement, centered on a young Shiraz merchant, 'Ali Muhammad, known to History as 'the Bab'. The Babi movement in turn had its roots in the heterodox Shaykhi sect of Shi'ite Islam. The Shaykhis had already got into trouble with some of the orthodox over the anti-literalist interpretation of certain Qur'anic doctrine by their founder, the Arab, Shaykh Ahmad of al-Ahsa. Shaykh Ahmad held, among other things, that such matters as heaven and hell, the resurrection of the body, and various ideas supported by taking certain verses of the Qur'an literally, had in fact a symbolic, not physical truth. In a still largely fundamentalist Islamic area of the world, these liberal ideas were innovatory enough; but another doctrine of Shaykh Ahmad, which he passed to his successor, Siyyid Kazim of Rasht, was the

imminent appearance of the promised one of Islam, to
Shi'ihs, the *'Qa'im'*.

To the Shi'ihs, the *Qa'im* meant the fulfilment of
their Faith's promise that the missing twelfth Imam, who
according to tradition had disappeared in the year 260
A.H. (873 A.D.), would return to them at the end of the
world. When the Imam returned he would, naturally, take for
himself the power he had left in the hands of his custodians,
the Shi'ite clergy. Needless to say, these clergy took a keen
interest in anybody foolish enough to claim the rank of
Qa'im.

First of all, 'Ali Muhammad was considered by his followers to be the 'gate' who would lead them to the hidden
Imam — hence his title of Bab (Arabic for 'gate'). The whole
question of the rank which the Bab claimed for himself is a
delicate one, however. Like the founder of Christianity, it
appears the Bab was often cryptic in his public utterances
about his station. But in private, to his first disciple, Mulla
Husayn of Bushihr, the Bab identified himself with the
promised one foretold by Shaykh Ahmad. This was on the
night of 22 May, 1844 — in the Muslim calendar, the year
was 1260, exactly 1,000 years since the death of the last
Imam.

What is clear from the bloodstained history of the Babi
movement is that the authorities civil and religious saw the
Bab as a threat to their own positions, and a heretic of Islam.
For it became clear eventually that the Bab *was* claiming to
be the *Qa'im*. In his writings — circulated among his followers
even whilst he was imprisoned — the Bab unmistakably
annulled the Islamic dispensation; and in his holy book, the
Bayan, evidently compared himself to the Prophet Muhammad. This was as outrageous in the eyes of orthodox Shi'ihs
as Christ's assumption of the rôle of Messiah had been to the
Jews; and their reaction was far more vicious. That this was
so was made even more sure by the defection of some of the
highest ranking clergy to the Bab's cause. At one point, in
1847, it even looked as though the young prophet would
march on the capital itself, and persuade the Shah to adopt
his religion.

Yet bloody and cruel as were the persecutions of Babis which reached their height between 1848 and 1852, the Bab remained serene and other-worldly in his outlook and behaviour. Though his followers perforce took up arms to defend themselves, he never encouraged a single act of violence; and though he was offered soldiers by the Governor of Isfahan, Manuchichr Khan, as a free escort to Tehran, he refused. He accepted imprisonment and eventual martyrdom from a firing squad in Tabriz, on July 9, 1850.

History accepts the Babis as heroic — Western diplomats and agents in Persia saw them as fanatic too. Wherever they assembled to defend themselves they embarrassed the authorities — putting to flight the Imperial Army itself, against all odds. Doubtless some were hotheads, but many seemed to be possessed of a remarkable faith and fortitude, and women and children joined with the menfolk to suffer the hardships of siege, battle, and the enemy's treachery and ghoulish methods of execution. In 1852, a handful of crazed Babis plotted the assassination of the Shah as a reprisal for the death of their leader, the Bab. Though the rest of their co-religionists had no hand in the attempt — which failed — they fell victim to the wrath of the Shah, his ministers, and the bloodlust of the clergy. Perhaps as many as twenty thousand Babis succumbed to the pogrom that ensued. The Comte Gobineau gave the following account of a few of these deaths:

> One saw that day in the streets and bazaars of Tehran a spectacle that the population will never forget. One saw, walking between staffs of executioners, children and women, with flesh gaping all over their bodies, with lighted wicks soaked in oil stuck in the wounds. The victims were dragged by cords and driven with whips. The children and women walked singing a verse, which says, 'In truth we come from God, and we return to Him.' Their voices rose piercingly in the middle of the profound silence of the mob; for the population of Tehran is neither bad-hearted nor much devoted to Islam. When one of the tortured people fell, he was forced to rise with blows from whips and prods from bayonets. If the loss of blood which ensued from the

wounds all over the body left him strength enough, he began to dance and shout with fervour, 'We belong to God, and we return to Him.' Some of the children expired *en route*. The executioners threw their bodies under the feet of their father and sister, who walked fiercely upon them, without looking.

When they arrived at the place of execution near the new gate, life was again offered to the victims if they would adjure their faith, and, though it seemed difficult, means were sought to intimidate them. The executioner hit upon the device of signing to a father that if he did not adjure he would cut the throat of his two sons upon his chest. These were two small boys, the eldest being fourteen, who, red with their own blood and with flesh scorched by the candles, listened unmoved. The father answered by lying down on the earth that he was ready, and the eldest of the boys, claiming his right of birth, begged to have his throat cut first. It is not impossible that the executioner refused him this last satisfaction. At last everything was ended, and the night fell upon a heap of mangled human remains. The heads were strung in bundles to the Posts of Justice, and all the dogs of the suburbs made their way to that side of town.

This day gave to the Bab more secret partisans than many preachings could have done.*

'Of no small account,' wrote Lord Curzon, in *Persia and the Persian Question*, '. . . must be the tenets of a creed that can awaken in its followers so rare and beautiful a spirit of self-sacrifice.' And he concurred with Gobineau that the persecution suffered by the Babis, far from diminishing their influence had caused them to increase in number.

One of the Babis, renowned in her own time among her own people as poetess and champion of woman's rights, achieved even greater fame in the outside world. This was Tahirih ('Pure One'), who suffered death in the holocaust that followed the attempt on the life of the Shah in 1852. From her childhood she was regarded as a prodigy, and she was also beautiful. Yet she was of a priestly family, and was married as was the custom in the patriarchal society of Persia,

* Gobineau, *Religions and Philosophies in Central Asia,* trans. Lorey and Sladen, *Queen things about Persia*, 315-316.

to a cousin. Against the conservatism of her father, uncle, and cousin, she argued the Bab's claim, and when summoned by her husband refused to return to him, giving as her reason his failure to embrace the Bab's cause. Such defiance of centuries of obscurantism could not go unpunished — Tahirih was eventually strangled with her scarf, and her body thrown down a well, which in turn was heeped with stones.

Tahirih had even shocked the supporters of the new religion: at one of their conferences she removed her veil in the midst of them. This is justifiably considered by Baha'i writers as an act of remarkable symbolic power — being no less than the inauguration of a new era in the lives of the women of the East. It is of significance when it is remembered that Islamic fundamentalists of today have charged Baha'is of practising prostitution. The doctrine of the equality of men and women which progressively freed the Baha'i women from the fetters of custom buttressed by Islamic tradition, is still of potent import in the Islamic world.

Yet this was not the only potentially explosive idea emerging from within the new religious community. Thirteen years after the death of the Bab, in 1863, a new figure stood out from the ranks of the Babis. This was Mirza Husayn Ali, called Baha'u'llah ('the Glory of God'), a nobleman from Mazindaran, and an erstwhile supporter of the Bab. His prominence among the exiled community of Persian Babis in Iraq (the Babis in Persia had suffered virtual suppression after 1852) reached the officials of the Ottoman Empire in Baghdad where he was living. Admirers came from Sulaymaniyyih, the mountainous region straddling both Iraq and Persia, where Baha'u'llah had dwelt for two years disguised as a Sufi *darvish*. Under the tutelage of Baha'u'llah, there grew up a revitalised community, and when he claimed to be the one promised by the Bab, the Babis accepted *en masse*, and renamed themselves Baha'is. Henceforth, the religion of the Bab was transformed into the religion of Baha'u'llah, the majority of Babis accepting that the earlier faith had achieved its fulfilment in the new one.

A great change brought about by Baha'u'llah was that the Baha'is became entirely peaceful. They no longer defended themselves when challenged and called upon to return to the Islamic fold. And soon certain teachings were made explicit which confirmed that while the Babis had constituted a great threat to the authorities on account of their zeal and fervour, the Baha'is were now to be instilled with doctrines that seriously embarrassed the orthodox mullas.

The most important example was the abolition of the rôle of clergy in the new religion. Baha'u'llah taught the need for independent investigation of truth. Such a principle if practised would at once circumvent the vested hold of the mujtahids, the doctors of Shi'ite Islam who had the power to make pronouncements over vast areas of practice and belief not covered by the Qur'an and the Traditions. In fact the whole monolith of Shi'ite law and custom, labyrinthine, cobwebbed and opaque, open only to those who had graduated from the seminaries or the carpeted environs of some erudite Shaykh, was at a word by-passed. No wonder the clergy took every opportunity to castigate the new movement, and move their congregations to its extirpation.

It is easy to miss the consternation Baha'i teaching caused among the Islamic doctors and mullas. Their reaction was to represent the Baha'is as accursed heretics — when what they really meant was that here was a revolutionary cause that cut the ground from under their own feet. They made common cause with the autocratic Shah; Baha'u'llah, they informed him, was preaching sedition against his throne, for had he not written in his book of laws (*Kitab-i-Akdas*) that kings should take the people into their counsel? Baha'u'llah wrote that kings derived their powers from the people, not from any absolute right!

It was not an easy matter to have Baha'u'llah executed as the Bab had been. His father had been a minister to the late Fath'Ali Shah, and though his own possessions had been largely seized or destroyed on his becoming a Babi, Baha'u'llah's character, together with his ancestry, made it difficult to do away with him. It was politic to have Baha'u'llah removed from Persia — though he was not spared four months in the pestilential Siyah-Chal ('black pit'), once a sewer, now an underground hollow where Babis were herded after the attempt on the life of the Shah, and from where most were taken to their execution.

An exile in Baghdad, the prominent Babi soon became frequented of officials and intelligentsia. The Persian Government became jealous, and egged on by the clerics whom Baha'u'llah had humiliated in their ignorance in Baghdad, the Shah entered into negotiations with the Sultan of Turkey. He spent three months in Istanbul, and was sent on to Edirne. From there he was packed off to desolate Acre, the very outpost of Ottoman domains, where he and his family and most ardent disciples could be left to rot.

The Baha'i Faith was thus transplanted from Persia to Palestine because the religious and secular authorities could not endure its politics. The Baha'i leader was no intriguer or enemy of Persia — he turned down offers of asylum in Russia and India from the Russian and British government representatives in Tehran and Baghdad respectively. Yet for all that what this exile obtained was power — power over the minds and hearts of thousands whom the clergy and government could not control. It was for this reason they hated his politics — they were motivated by crass jealousy. Baha'u'llah was also responsible for establishing the non-political character of his religion. He wrote: 'In every country where any of this people (i.e. Baha'is) reside, they must behave towards the government of that country with loyalty, honesty and truthfulness.' The Babis had not set out to overthrow the state, but religious affairs are interwoven with politics in the Islamic world. There was no such thing as an organised political opposition in those days; the masses had no political voice. But the new religious cause became associated with reform, and it was met with repression on a wide scale.

Those Babis who escaped the holocaust of 1852 and settled in Iraq suffered demoralisation before Baha'u'llah's rise to eminence and assumption of outright leadership. His doing this was accompanied by the major schism in the movement — for his half-brother, Mirza Yahya, was the appointed head of the Babis, even though he was cowardly and despised by most of his flock. This schism involved the Babi-Baha'is unwittingly in political matters, for Yahya's small body of supporters, the Azalis, engaged in intrigue with both Ottoman and Persian authorities in Baghdad and Tehran. As late as the first decade of the twentieth century, when Abdu'l-Baha, the son of Baha'u'llah, was leader of the Baha'i community, these old enemies combined with disaffected members of the Baha'u'llah's family, and represented the Baha'i community in Palestine as a political threat to the Sultan.

European diplomats in Persia from the first sent dispatches to their governments mentioning the new Faith. 'The opinion shared by almost all of the European colony in Tihran in 1850-52 seems to have been that the Baha'is were socialists, communists and anarchists.'* But this view had to be seen in the light of the disturbances in Europe of this period. The Romantic Age had culminated in the year of revolutions — 1848. The spectre of Communism, according to Marx and Engels in the *Communist Manifesto,* haunted the capitals of Europe. In fact this was looking forward to the period 1870-1914, when the Paris Commune was fresh in all minds; the Babis were represented as nihilists, pantheists, and sharers of everything, including wives, by Europeans who probably retained a memory of the millennialist sects in the West, such as the St. Simonians.

The notion that the Babi-Baha'is were in the pay of British and Russian imperialism (both at the same time!) is really too ludicrous to answer, but it says more about the people who entertain it than it does about any historical reality. It is of course a common ploy to brand one's enemies as being in the pay of an outside power, and therefore traitors. Such ideas reflect the xenophobia of the ignorant, but that they have held sway in Iran for so long, and have been lately repeated, alongside the newer charges that Baha'is are Zionists and agents of United States Imperialism, is testimony to the lack of ingenuity of the fanatics and the cupidity of those who believe them.

The failure of the European diplomats to properly focus the truth about the new movement was however no reason to

* Moojan Momen, *The Babi and Baha'i Religion 1844-1944,*
  p. 5.

prevent them from intervening to plead tolerance on behalf
of the hapless victims of execution and torture. The British
and Russian ministers in Tehran in 1852 made a joint appeal
to the Shah to stop the pogrom of Babis following the
attempt on his life. They were unsuccessful. *The Times* of 13
October of that year included a report entitled: 'How they
punish treason in Persia', displaying Western distaste for the
cruelty of the Oriental: 'We mentioned a few days since the
attempt against the Shah of Persia. We now learn that Hajee
Suleiman Khan, accused as instigator of the crime, was
seized, his body carefully drilled with a knife in parts which
would not at the moment cause death; pieces of lighted
candles were then introduced into the holes, and thus illu-
minated, [he was] carried in procession through the bazaar,
and finally conveyed to the town gates, and there cleft in
twain like a fat ram.'

What little Western diplomats could do for the Baha'is was
welcome as the only source from where succour could come.
Then as later, no voice was raised by the inhabitants of Iran
against the unjust treatment of Baha'is. After 1883, a small
community of Baha'i merchants went to settle in Russia, over
the border from Persia at Ishkabad. They sought the freedom
of worship they believed a Christian government would give
them, and were at first so favourably received by the authorities that the Shah became jealous and communicated with
the Russian Government. In a report from a member of the
British legation in Tehran, the British Foreign Office was
informed: 'The Russian Govt. has now reassured the Shah's
Govt. on the subject and state they do not intend to show
the Babis any favour.' Thus was the Baha'i community of
Ishkabad unwittingly victim to politics.

Baha'u'llah built up, in spite of his exile, and in spite of
the periodic persecutions suffered by the Baha'is in Persia,
who had no recourse to justice, an expanding religious
community. After the death of the Bab, famine and disease
raged in Persia. An earthquake devastated the prophet's
native city of Shiraz. Cholera later broke out. An historian
writes: 'It is not improbable that these visitations and the
consequent demonstration of both gross inefficiency and

corruption in the Government, as well as the hypocrisy and worldliness of the Shi'ih divines, were catalytic factors that created a general feeling of unrest in the country and contributed to the rapid spread of the Baha'i religion on the one hand, and prepared the minds of the people for political agitation towards liberal reform on the other.'*

That the Baha'i Community as it had now developed was neither a threat to the state nor a bizarre organization of heretical zealots was at last recognized by a European diplomatic writer, Lord Curzon, in his *Persia and the Persian Question* of 1892. He wrote:

> From the facts that Babism in its earliest years found itself in conflict with the civil powers, and that an attempt was made by Babis upon the life of the Shah, it has been wrongly inferred that the movement was political in origin and Nihilist in character. It does not appear from a study of the writings of either the Bab or his successors, that there is any foundation for such a suspicion. The persecution of the government very early drove the adherents of the new creed into an attitude of rebellion; and in the exasperation produced by the struggle, and by the ferocious brutality with which the rights of conquest were exercised by the victors, it was not surprising if fanatical hands were found ready to strike the sovereign down. At the present time the Babis are equally loyal with any other subjects of the Crown. Nor does there appear any greater justice in the charges of socialism, communism, and immorality, that have so freely been levelled at the youthful persuasion . . . The only communism known to and recommended by him [the Bab] was that of the New Testament and the early Christian Church, viz., the sharing of goods in common by members of the faith, and the exercise of alms-giving, and an ample charity. The charge of immorality seems to have arisen partly from the malignant inventions of opponents, partly from the much greater freedom claimed for women by the Bab, which in the oriental mind is scarcely dissociable from profligacy of conduct
> . . .
> . . . The Bab and Beha in their writings have enjoined the disuse of the veil, the abolition of divorce, poly-

* Momen, op. cit., p. 243.

gamy, and concubinage, in other words of the harem, and greater liberty of action for the female sex.
. . . Broadly regarded, Babism may be defined as a creed of charity, almost of common humanity. Brotherly love, kindness to children, courtesy combined with dignity, sociability, hospitality, freedom from bigotry, friendliness even to Christians, are included in its tenets.

Curzon clearly felt that the challenge the new religion held out to the old order in Persia resided in its ethical superiority, not in any political pretentions its enemies might attribute to it. What struck him was the signs of purity and renewal he found among the Baha'is, and this led him to overestimate their number (he thought there were a million of them), and to prophesy for them a remarkable future. ('If Babism continues to grow at its present rate of progression, a time may conceivably come when it will oust Mohammedanism from the field in Persia . . .')

Yet despite the favourable opinion of Curzon, and the championing of the Babi cause by Gobineau, and later, E.G. Browne of Cambridge, the ostrasizing of the Baha'is in Persia frequently broke out into outright violence. In the Isfahan-Najafabad area the Baha'is had powerful enemies among the clergy, emboldened by the attitude of the Governor of Isfahan, Zillu's-Sultan, who deemed it expedient to cover his political ambitions with occasional pogroms against the outcast community. 'Indeed, his Governorship was inaugurated by a general persecution of tbe Baha'is within a few days of his arrival.'* The Baha'is were arrested or forced to flee in their hundreds, and a contemporary observer, a missionary in Isfahan, reported that:

> . . . the Shaik preached publically in the great Mosque that the blood of all those arrested was *hallal* (i.e. lawful) for him to shed, and that their wives and daughters and property were at the mercy of the Mahomedans to do what they liked to them.

This time events were prevented from taking a more

* Momen, op. cit., pp. 269-270.

bloody course with the help of the intervention of the British Minister in Tehran. Momen writes:

> In planning this outburst against the Baha'is, Shaykh Muhammad-Baqir leading mujtahid of Isfahan and the Zillu's-Sultan sought to prevent any means whereby the Baha'is could appeal to Tihran against the persecution. Thus the Telegraph Office and the Postmaster were instructed to refuse any petitions from the Baha'is, while a special watch was kept at the city gates. The Baha'is, however, managed to smuggle a messenger out of the city who rode in haste to Kashan. Here he mobilized tbe Baha'is of the town to march to the Telegraph Office, and thus succeeded in getting a message to the central Government. Eventually orders arrived from Tihran that the persecution must cease.*

Five years after this episode, in 1879, the Zillu's-Sultan allowed the 'high priest' of Isfahan (Imam-Jumih) to have put to death two Baha'i merchants to whom he owed money. This squalid affair earned the cleric contempt in the eyes of European observers in the city, and the two innocent Baha'is, who were brothers, were accorded a special rank as martyrs among their co-religionists.

A decade later, the Muslim clerics again agitated for the execution of a Baha'i merchant on the grounds of his religion. The same missionary who had intervened in the arrests of 1874 wrote in his annual report for 1889: '*Persecutions* — last autumn, a short time before our return from England, a very respectable man, a native of Abadeh, was put to death by the Mohammedan priests in Ispahan in a most cruel manner for being a Babi, and the poor body was most barbarously mutilated and burnt. A fanatical priesthood, like a man-eating tiger, having once tasted human blood, thirsts for more.'

On two more occasions, in 1889 and 1890, Babis in the Isfahan area were driven from their homes at the instigation of the mullas and left unprotected by the Zillu's-Sultan. Once again the case of the Baha'is was argued by British Officials in

* Momen, op. cit., pp. 272-273.

Tehran, on humanitarian grounds. Fleeing Baha'i villagers
from Sidih, on the latter occasion, were attacked by a hostile crowd, as a member of the British legation in Isfahan
reported:

> About two miles from their home they were met by a
> party of some two thousand people; they themselves
> numbering about thirty. The attacking party was armed
> with spades, clubs and knives and was headed by Seyed
> Ali, the religious chief of the Sehdé community. He
> loudly proclaimed a 'Jahad' or religious war and shouted
> out — 'We have no king but Agha Nedjefy; he is our
> king and representative of the Imam and I am his
> lieutenant: kill these infidels and blot out their names.'
>
> The people at once attacked, killing six and badly
> wounding several, one of whom soon afterwards died of
> his wounds.

Aqa Najafi, in whose name these acts were committed, was
the son of Shaykh Muhammad-Baqir, the Shaykhu'l-Islam of
Isfahan, and an infamous persecutor of Baha'is. The property
of the persecuted was easy plunder, for none ever defended
themselves.

Seven Baha'is were killed in Yazd in 1891 in a course of
events that typifies the persecution of Baha'is as scapegoats
in Persia, then and thereafter almost to the present day. An
agitator in the cause of the before-mentioned Zillu's-Sultan
was apprehended in Tehran in the process of intriguing for
the replacement of the Shah by his master. The Zillu's-Sultan
was so frightened that in order to divert attention he had his
son, Prince Jalalu'd-Dawla, set afoot a persecution of Baha'is
in and around Yazd. The British Chargé d'Affaires in Tehran,
in a report to the British Foreign Minister in London, throws
some light on this incredible manoeuvre: 'in an interview
which I had yesterday with the Amin-us-Sultan, His Highness
informed me in great confidence that His Royal Highness the
Zil-us-Sultan had written to the Shah and had taken great
credit to himself ... for the energetic manner in which the
Babis of Yezd had been suppressed and the true interests of
Islam had been protected ...'

The innocent victims of political legerdemain, the Baha'is were themselves next accused of being responsible for the assassination of the Shah in 1896. In a letter to *The Times* discountenancing this view, E.G. Browne echoed Lord Curzon's opinion that since the attempted assassination of 1852 — which the majority of Babis had had no sympathy with anyway — the new Faith had proved itself loyal to the government of the Shah, and free from any malice against him. The Shah had lately shown an inclination to temper the persecution of Baha'is by the mullas, and the Baha'is had the worst to fear from any anarchy resulting from his death.

The Baha'is lost their sustainer when Baha'u'llah died in Bahji, near Acre, in 1892. Baha'u'llah had transformed the religious movement into a universalist, pacific Faith, whose followers embodied a high standard of conduct, a disinclination to involve themselves in any form of politics, and a resignation to sporadic persecutions which often earned the admiration of independent observers. In the later years of his exile in Palestine, the focus of the Baha'i Faith became fully fixed on the Holy Land, where Shi'ite Islam held no sway. In Persia itself, substantial conversions had taken place among Jews and Zoroastrians, and the Baha'i Faith was being established, as it is today, as the most sizeable non-Muslim religion in the land. Christian missionaries in Persia and Palestine were beginning to take notice of a movement which they could see had transformed traditional Muslim antipathy towards Christians into a position where it seemed to stand as mediator between Islam and Christianity. It was a Christian missionary — albeit a hostile one — who first introduced the Baha'i religion to a Western audience in a reference he made at the Chicago World Parliament of Religions, on 23 September, 1893.

The next stage in the fortunes of the Baha'is in Persia saw them drawn against their will into the storm of revolutionary politics. The struggle for reform from within Persia inevitably expressed itself in overt political action in the first decade of the twentieth century. The Qajar dynasty remained reactionary to the last, and the battles that ensued between legitimists and reformers invoked periods of civil war in which the

Baha'is suffered for not taking sides. The apolitical stance of
the Baha'is, which had been strongly reiterated by the new
head of the community, Abdu'l-Baha, who remained a
prisoner in Palestine, meant that both sides in the struggle
attacked them, and represented them as being on the opposite side.

The matter was complicated by the decidedly political
activities of the Azalis, who supported the reformists and had
indeed long been agitating against the Shah. Both Baha'is and
Azalis were still referred to as Babis, and in the West many
were under the misapprehension that the Babis were the chief
instigators of the reform movement. In a sense there were
grounds for this beyond the obvious reason that the Azali-
Babis were pro-reform: E.G. Browne saw the constitutionalist
struggle as the means of revitalising Persia, and believing
the Babi movement to be identified with the same goal,
he was disappointed when the Baha'is remained aloof.
Reactionary mullas are said to have confronted revolutionary
mobs with copies of the Qur'an in one hand and Baha'u'llah's
Kitab-i-Akdas in the other, and demanded to know which
they were supporting. Indeed, there was no question but that
Baha'u'llah's writings advocated a form of consultative
democracy; one of the most prominent reformists, Haji
Shaykhu'r-Rais, a Qajar Prince and eloquent orator, actually
became a Baha'i. He was forbidden active involvement in the
political agitation by Abdu'l-Baha, but his political allegiance
was too well known; his conversion to the Baha'i Faith was
revealed, two of his fellow reformists were also Baha'is, and it
wanted only this to give the anti-Baha'i, Aqa Najafi, opportunity to ferment more trouble for the Baha'is. Several
hundred took refuge in the Russian consulate in that city.

Thus although the teachings of the new Faith appeared to
support the progressive cause, the non-involvement in politics
of the Baha'is was even stronger — when it was broken by a
tiny minority, it got the community as a whole into great
trouble. The wisdom of the founders of the Faith becomes
apparent: if the Baha'is became active in politics, whatever
the cause, they risked the well-being of their fellow believers
elsewhere. If the Baha'is joined the progressive cause in one

area, or indeed one country, it would be sure to have repercussions in different places where variant political conditions
prevailed. Moreover, Adbu'l-Baha made it quite clear in a
letter of this period on this theme, that the Baha'is wished to
bring together the various factions rather than cause division.
The universalism of Baha'u'llah's teachings envisaged a united
human race, not a discordant one. So Abdu'l-Baha:

> From the very beginning of the Revolution it was
> constantly enjoined that the Friends of God should
> stand aside from this struggle and war and contest, and
> should seek to reconcile the Court and Nation . . .

Yet this standing above politics incurred its own penalties,
as the history of the Baha'i Community continually demon-
strates.

The Baha'is who fled from the rage of Aqa Najafi's mob
into the protection of the Russian consulate were faced with
a howling mob raised by a forged telegram purported to be
from the Shah, giving *carte blanche* to the destruction of the
Baha'is. When the mob seemed to have dispersed, the reluc-
tant Babis, now an embarrassment to the Russian Acting
Consul, were obliged to leave. However, many of the mob
remained hiding in waiting and groups of the Baha'is were
attacked with sticks, knives and metal chains. The Baha'is
were exposed to the ferocity of their enemies in the vicinity
of the consulate, and returning to their homes. Some were
badly injured, at least one died. Finally, two Baha'i brothers,
merchants of the town, were arrested, extracted from prison
before they could be dealt with officially, and lynched by
ruffians. A.L.M. Nicholas wrote:

> . . . Siyyid Husayn and a group of barefoot ruffians
> extracted the two brothers from prison and martyred
> them in such a manner that even their enemies wept.
> They cut them to pieces with blows from sticks, rocks
> and knives in the caravanserai of the Yazdis.
> They tied a tope to their feet and Haji Hadi was taken
> to the Maydan-i-Shah and burnt, Haji Husayn suffered
> the same fate in the Maydan-i-Kuhnih.

One Anglican missionary included in his account the remarks of a fellow missionary who had been an eye-witness: ' 'The horrors of the day you have doubtless heard, the mutilated body of Haji Hadi lies not fifty yards from my house on a dung heap ...' ' So ended another pogrom initiated by the leading Shi'ite clerics of Isfahan.

Yet this was nothing compared to the full scale onslaught unleashed against the Baha'is in Yazd, next month, June 1903. The coming of a new Imam-Jumih to the city sparked off two days of rampaging in the streets in quest of Baha'is. The Governor was this time really powerless to do anything. A Baha'i shopkeeper was murdered in these first disturbances which spread into neighbouring villages. When they were renewed after a temporary lull, it was to see the worst pogrom of Baha'is for many years. Dispatches from the British agent to Tehran revealed the growing alarm of the Europeans, who might at first have feared for their own safety. The Prime Minister in Tehran, the unpopular Aminu's-Sultan, received a note from the British Legation there expressing its concern. Telegrams were sent by the same source to the Governor of India and the Foreign Office in London. Worst fears were soon too terribly realized. Day by day Baha'is were being killed: 'twelve babis killed and bodies maltreated many babi houses raided plundered ... Today again rabble have searched out and killed babis dragging mutilated bodies through streets ... Governor is absolutely without authority ...' (telegram of British agent in Yazd to British Minister in Tehran, 27 June, 1903). Another telegram (29 June to Tehran): 'Yesterday disturbance continued and the Governor killed two Babis brought to him. The mob also killed two or three dragging their bodies through the town. ... a leading Mujtehed enjoined the populace yesterday to desist from plundering and bring all Babis to Governor or Mujtehed for judgement ...' In a letter of report sent on the 3 July: 'Disturbances of varying magnitude are repeated at most of the surrounding villages and it is estimated that about forty Babis have lost their lives in Yezd and forty to fifty in the district since the commencement of these disturbances.' Again the British Minister in Tehran approached the

Persian Prime Minister urging him to send reinforcements to Yazd to quell the situation.

News of the massacres of Yazd reached the London and *New York Times*. The following are extracts from a long report of a missionary, Miss Jessie Briggs, written at the height of the troubles:

> *On Monday June 15* we heard a Babi had been killed in Yezd and some of our Babi friends came to us in distress for advice ... *On June 17* we heard of 2 more men being killed — one living next door to one of our converts ... The wife of the man was also badly hurt by women beating her and biting her about the hands and face ... *On Wed. June 24* ... We had heard that a Sayid from Isfahan had come to town (Imam Jumeh) and it was he who was stirring up the people ... *Sat. June 27* ... one of our 2 women converts was brought in badly hurt during yesterday's mob. One of her sons, a Babi had gone as usual to a small weaving factory close by, and someone told her he was in danger. With this she hastened to him but got into the house only to see him killed before her eyes. In her efforts to protect him she got badly beaten on her head and arm and leg, one finger broken and dislocated and another nearly cut off ... One of her brothers was killed and also a small child only a few months old ...
>
> *Sunday June 28* ... Quite in the evening a note came from the Prince requesting we should get rid of all the Babis [whom the missionaries had been hiding from the mob].... A command has also gone forth that searching of homes is to stop, and that any Babi found is to be taken up to the Castle and there judged. The judgement seems simply to make the prisoner curse the Bab, which if he refuses to do, is punished by death, probably being blown from a cannon's mouth. Their modes of killing these poor hunted Babis, have been dreadful. Some have been beaten and stoned to death, others shot over and over again, and others cut to pieces ...
>
> *Monday June 29* we admitted an old woman about 70 ... into our hospital. She had a bad knife or sword cut to the elbow joint and other hurts ...

Such reports indicate the overall pattern of persecution; the high-ranking cleric arrives and his presence inspires —

wittingly — the mob, already at fever-pitch against the
hapless 'heretics' after events in Isfahan, to kill and plunder
at will. The authorities are forced to watch, but take advantage of a lull to re-establish their writ and give the persecutions official sanction, curbing the anarchy by undertaking
executions themselves. These are administered in the now
established fashion: victims presented with the option of
recanting their faith or being put to death. Thus the collusion
of clergy, mob and government authorities in the persecution
of Baha'is in 1903.

During the first two decades of the twentieth century, in
the unsettled times that faced Persia, the Baha'is suffered
recurrent harassment, particularly in outlying areas. Whereas
persecutions such as that seen at Yazd were spectacular
occurrences, the general pressure placed upon Baha'is was
more invidious. In the pogroms so far discussed the tendency
to treat the Baha'is foully merely as a means of releasing the
worst instincts in human nature can be seen clearly. Moreover
the barbarity of the persecutors is a recurring theme in
European reports from first-hand witnesses, and tells much
about the level of enlightenment in Persian society. On an
everyday basis, however, the position of the Baha'is could
scarcely be said to be any easier. 'The Baha'is derived little
benefit from the Constitutional Movement. When the Constitution itself was drafted it did not safeguard their rights, and
when the electoral laws were introduced in 1906 and 1909
there were specific provisions that prevented them from even
being able to vote.'* In practice, this meant that the Baha'is
had no legal rights (Article 5 specifically referred to apostates
from Islam and precluded them from any enfranchisement)
and were thus, as before, open to all kinds of harassment.
This was to be the way with every subsequent change of
regime or head of state: thus Reza Shah inaugurated the
Pahlavi dynasty with systematic discriminatory measures
aimed at removing from Baha'is any legal protection. They
remained second-class citizens throughout his reign, and the
reign of his son, Mohammed Reza. The Islamic Revolution of

* Momen, op. cit., pp. 367-368.

1979, and the Islamic Constitution it created, once again saw the Baha'is excluded from all recognition.

With the fall of the last Qajar in 1925, the rôle of the clergy in Persia waned. The new secular state took over the role of oppressor, though, with one outstanding exception, not with overt force as before. The Baha'is had most to fear from the bloodthirsty mob — that perennial agent of malice in barely civilized countries, such as Iran, as Persia now became known. In 1926 anti-Baha'i riots broke out in Jahrum, provoked by a fanatical Mujtahid whose father had been a renowned enemy of the Baha'is. These were manipulated by one Ismail Khan, a political opportunist, who took the chance such a disturbance offered to have his recent defeat in the elections for the Majlis (Parliament) overlooked. Some eight Baha'is were murdered with the now customary savagery of the fanatical mob. This time, however, a new factor entered events. The Baha'is of the Western world, hearing of the persecutions of their co-religionists, lobbied the diplomatic sources, particularly those in Tehran, and telegrams of complaint were sent to the Shah, causing him to instruct postal and telegraph offices not to accept petitions from Baha'is. Following on this new mode of intervention, the British High Commission in Iraq received a petition to use its influence on behalf of the Baha'is in Iran, by the National Spiritual Assembly of the Baha'is of Iraq. This was the beginning of the interest taken by the growing Baha'i World Community in the privations and suffering of their co-religionists in Iran.

But how much pressure were foreign governments prepared to exert on another sovereign country over affairs within that country's own domains? The new revolutionary regime in the Soviet Union was itself engaged in extirpating religious practice, and applied pressure on the Baha'is in the later 'twenties as it did to all religions in its territory. It was even suggested by British diplomats in Iran that the Russian Consul-General in Iran was behind the Jahrum disturbances. The protecting hand of the British themselves in Iran was undoubtedly motivated by their long-held concern for human rights. But the British too had their interests, and wishing to see a stable Iran they would not wish to identify with any particular group in the country against the wishes of the Shah. This could be seen behind King George V's response to a pamphlet presented him by Baha'is in London in 1911. Would it be politic for him to acknowledge it in view of the unsettled state of Persia at that time? The Foreign Office gave its opinion: 'The movement in question ... may be harmless enough in itself as a religious development but its history shows that neither under its religious nor under its political aspect has it ever been regarded with favour by the Turkish or the Persian Government. There is always ... the possibility that an acknowledgement ... may be interpreted as an encouragement ... any supposed encouragement might cause annoyance in Turkey and Persia, it would appear preferable that none be sent.' So much for the charge that the Babi-Baha'i Faith was created by, and in the pay of, the British Government.

After the persecutions of 1926 no organised pogrom of Baha'is took place for nearly thirty years. This may be attributable to the decline of influence of the Shi'ite divines, but this did not mean the Baha'is enjoyed toleration. Baha'i marriages were refused recognition. Baha'i literature was banned and Baha'i meetings forbidden. Civil service ranks were subject to purges of the Baha'is — it being obligatory to state one's religion on application to the service, and orders existed that forbade recruitment of Baha'is. Occasionally, a Baha'i would be murdered somewhere. And in 1934 the State closed Baha'i schools, including the renowned Tarbiyat schools for girls and boys respectively in Tehran. Only a half of the students attending these schools were Baha'is, but the Ministry of Education took as its pretext that the schools had been 'closed without reason' the previous year. These closures were to mark Baha'i holy days, which according to their religious law were to involve suspension of work. The Baha'is closed the schools as usual on the holy day marking the anniversary of the Bab's death, knowing that the Government would thereafter not allow them to re-open.

The reason for this discrimination from an entirely secular power might seem at first sight less easy to understand than the clergy-inspired pogroms. In fact under the 1909 Constitution Islam remained the acknowledged religion of the state. The other religious minorities were at least afforded recognition, though such was the standard of observation of human rights within Iran that Christian, Jew and Zoroastrian could hardly feel themselves free from discrimination. A sizeable proportion of Zoroastrians left Iran before and during the civil wars. Jews would later tread the route to Palestine. The Baha'i Community meanwhile had passed the aggregate number of the other three minorities together — moreover, Baha'is had always drawn from all sections of the nation. The Baha'is were represented in the lowliest peasant communities and the higher strata of society at the same time. Governments could trust them — even while they bowed easily enough to popular prejudice when it suited them — because Baha'is, they knew, would be loyal to their authority.

That the loyalty Baha'is paid to the state out of obedience to the teachings of their religion rather than political preference, paid them no dividends at times of popular unrest, the events of 1955 attest. The whole episode reveals how deeply prejudice and hatred against the Baha'is had rooted itself in Iranian society, and how cynically this feeling could be manipulated by the political authorities when they considered it suited them. During the month of Ramadan, the Islamic month of fasting, a wide-ranging attack was launched against the Iranian Baha'i community. Shaykh Muhammad Taqi Falsafi, at his Tehran mosque, preached sermons against the 'false religion' daily. Further, he was able to disseminate his views more widely over the radio in an hourly space he had at his command. Private homes, places of business, and institutions of the Baha'is were plundered and looted; the House of the Bab, foremost Baha'i holy place in Iran, was partly demolished. Inevitably, given the passions aroused, and without a protecting hand to restrain them, mobs entered on an orgy of rape, murder, and pillage. Cemeteries were mutilated, and the corpses of Baha'is disinterred. Villagers were boycotted by suppliers, abductions and forced marriages occurred. But most symbolic of all, the Baha'i National Centre in Tehran, with its imposing dome, was taken over by police, army and clergy.

As the *Guardian* reported on 13 August, 1955: 'The National Baha'i Spiritual Centre in the capital city of Tehran was
occupied by troops. The magnificent dome was ripped to
pieces and reduced to its steel structure.' A contemporary
photograph shows high-ranking army officers wielding the axe,
flanked by a robed cleric — Falsafi himself. As in the case of
the Jahrum pogrom, the international Baha'i Community, now
on a far larger scale, apprised governments and international
agencies of what was going on. The international media carried
the news, and eminent figures registered their disapproval of
the Iranian authorities. In a letter to *The Times*, 3 September,
1955, Arnold Toynbee wrote: 'The Baha'is have a particularly
strong claim to be tolerated, because non-violence is one of
the cardinal principles of their religion.'

The Baha'is next appealed to the United Nations in the
name of the Human Rights Charter, to which the Iranian
Government was signatory; by August, 1955, the Government
of the Shah finally took a hand to intervene, and orders were
sent to restore to the Baha'is their centres and civil rights. But
a year later, it was again necessary for the Baha'is to appeal to
the United Nations, and this time the appeal had its effect.
The House of the Bab — the most holy Baha'i shrine in Iran —
was returned to its owners. The violent passions aroused by
the Shi'ite clergy died down. This too, like virtually all of the
previous progroms, had been their work. The license they had
gained from the Government had been a temporary one,
facilitated by anti-Baha'i feeling within the Shah's cabinet, led
by the future creator of SAVAK, then Military-Governor of
Tehran, General Teimour Bakhtiar.

For the entire period we have reviewed — 1844 to 1955 —
the Baha'i Community in Iran, and its precursor, the Babi
Community, had been more or less at the mercy of the two
powers of government and clergy. The most vicious pogrom
of all — the 1852 massacre of Babis — had been initiated by the
Shah himself, but the more usual pattern, as we have seen, was
for persecutions to begin with incendiary sermons on the part
of the Shi'ite clergy, that in turn fermented the mob to wreak
vengeance on a more or less defenceless minority. Help was

forthcoming intermittently from Christian missionaries and from Western agencies, often representing the interests of the British and Russian Governments. Sometimes these offices had effect, for the influence of these two powers in Persia was large. Yet all too often, help only came when the pogroms had already spent their force, and many victims lay either dead, or grievously wounded and stripped of their livelihoods. And when outside help did avail, it only went to fan the hatred of the enemy, who accused the outcasts of being agents of the foreign powers. The weakness of the central government also meant that unscrupulous Governors had a free reign to further their ambitions which could involve using the Baha'is as scapegoats to curry favour with the populace or clergy.

When Reza Khan instituted a stronger, more centralised government, the discrimination against Baha'is took a less overt, more bureaucratic form. Baha'is were made second-class citizens, whose rights were uncertain, and whose recourse to justice depended upon the velleities of the magistrate. Their position had not so much been improved as placed in abeyance. It is true that the Pahlavi monarchs had made themselves enemies of the Shi'ite clergy, the traditional persecutors of the Baha'is, and this relieved the pressure somewhat. However, new factors were now acquiring an increasing importance; as the twentieth century, with its secularizing, modernising trends, spread its influence in Iran, the Baha'is, the Shi'ite clerics, and the political forces around the State, prepared themselves for a more radical interaction. This process gathered momentum in the years of the Shah's dictatorship, that became established in the 1960s.

CHAPTER TWO

Baha'is under the Shah

In 1955 the attack on the Baha'i Community was led by a
cleric, and this represented a rare unison between the Shi'ite
clergy and the Pahlavi Government. A recent study of the
relationship of these two powers within Iran suggests that the
Government was glad to give Falsafi the opportunity to
attack the Baha'is, as at that time, following the period of
uncertainty after the coup against Mossadeq in 1953, the
Government wished to placate the right-wing clergy-led
elements in the country.* The attitude of the authorities
towards the Baha'is during the rest of the Shah's reign is of
particular interest when it is remembered how the Islamic
Government of Ayatollah Khomeini has repeated accused the
Baha'is of being in league with the Shah.

Baha'i sources claim that their members suffered disabili-
ties through the reign of the Shah. They claim that between
1957 and 1962 the Baha'is were 'condemned to a semi-
clandestine existence'. They instance the erasure of all
references to the Baha'is from the history books. A non-
Baha'i source reports that a high official in the Iranian
Government in 1955 told the United Nations there were no
Baha'is in Iran.† Official intoleration, maintain the Baha'is,
made entry of Baha'is into the army, civil service and teaching profession, not accepted — although this was not always
enforced. During the anti-Government demonstrations of
1963, Baha'is were again singled out for attack, this time by

* M.J. Fisher, *Iran: From Religious Dispute to Revolution*,
  p. 187.
† ibid.

the rioters. In 1972, say the Baha'is, the Government implemented a tax on Baha'i properties — in practice, the holy
places of the Faith, a heritage built up over the years by
charitable donations. Against this more or less official discrimination must be added the indubitable fact that the
Baha'is did not join the Shah's Rastakhiz Party when this was
founded in 1975, as it offended their scruples of not becoming involved in politics.

Indeed the non-political character of the Baha'i Faith and
its institutions during the period of the Shah cannot be
seriously called into doubt. Further to this, the association
Baha'is are continually being accused of having with Israel,
and therefore Zionism, is of a completely innocent character.
The Baha'i World Centre was established in Palestine by
accident of history long before the declaration of the State of
Israel. During the Shah's reign Baha'is made no secret of the
fact they were visiting the Holy Shrines of their Faith situa-
ted on Mount Carmel, as the Baha'i equivalent of the Islamic
hadj or pilgrimage. Neither was there any covering of the
donations that individuals made towards the rearing of the
celebrated Baha'i edifices on the slopes of the mountain.

In fact, the international dimensions of the Baha'i Faith
have been completely misunderstood within Iran itself. The
universalism of Baha'i tenets has either been misconstrued, or
distorted by opponents of the Baha'is there. Those Baha'is
who did become involved in politics against the commands of
their own Faith were expelled from the ranks of the Baha'is.*
Moreover, the charge that is made that Ministers in the Shah's
Government were Baha'is is not correct. Politicians named
include the Shah's Prime Minister for twelve years, Abbas
Hoveyda, and another Minister, Mansour Rouhani. In both
cases the individuals concerned came from families where one
or both parents were Baha'is, but as religion in the Baha'i
Faith is not determined by birth, but the election of the
individual himself at the age of maturity, it cannot be claimed

---

* For example, General Sani'i, who was instructed by the
NSA of Iran not to accept the post of War Minister in the
Shah's Cabinet, but did so.

that either were Baha'is. Neither ever became members of the
Baha'i Community, but as their families were associated with
the Baha'i Faith, their enemies branded them with this per-
suasion as well.* Powerful figures within the Iranian economy
were Baha'is however. Among them was Habib Sabet, builder
of the first Pepsi Cola factory in Iran, and a millionaire.
Sabet, and a few other rich Baha'is, like the banker and
financier, Hojabr Yazdani, can hardly be said to have done
the standing of their Faith any good by the ostentatious
dealings they were involved in during the periods of expan-
sion in the Iranian capitalist economy. Had they been serious
Baha'is they would have been aware that the founder of the
Baha'i Religion forbade both excessive wealth and poverty.
But to take them as representatives of the Baha'i Faith would
be unjust, since the Baha'i Faith has a recognized organization and institutions which should be considered its true
representation.

The prominence of individual Baha'is under the Shah
could also be attributed to the reliability and good character
of some of them. General 'Ali-Muhammad Khademi, head of
Iran Air, could not be criticized for his integrity. Other
Baha'is too served their country loyally. The stimulus for
education and striving within the Baha'i Faith is undoubtedly
behind the success of many Baha'is of the calibre of Professor
Hakim. Every community can display within its ranks exam-
ples good and not so good; enemies of the Baha'is instance
those who were not so good. Yet had the Baha'i Community
collectively had the degree of power the present authorities
in Iran maintain it had under the previous regime, it seems
peculiar that the Baha'is were unable to remove the definite
official and unofficial stigma that seemed to attach to the
name.

The Baha'is did come to be represented in the middle and
higher strata of society in non-political positions. The reasons

* Unfortunately for Hoveyda, he was never able to live down
  the charge that he was a Baha'i, even though he pains-
  takingly carried out the Islamic *hadj*, and even advertised
  his allegiance to Islam in newspapers.

for this are to be found both within the strong bias toward
education to be found in the Baha'i Faith, and the nature of
the Shah's regime itself. On the one hand, many Baha'is built
for themselves businesses and careers virtually from scratch;
on the other, the political dictatorship of the Shah, which
allowed no political involvement among the middle classes,
but encouraged a high level of economic individualism, suited
the hard-working, quietist character of the Baha'is. Thus the
Baha'is were never collaborationist in any active political
sense, but they had advantage of the economic situation to
the extent their personal exertions allowed.

This acceptance of circumstances can hardly be called
seriously reprehensible. As for the charge that it constituted
treasonous behaviour, Prime Minister Bazargan, for the
Islamic Republic, on 25 April 1979, reassured the army in
these terms: 'Officers and soldiers cannot be accused of
treason purely because they served under the Shah. We are all
guilty of having cooperated, willingly or not, with the old
regime.'

The Islamic Revolutionary regime has not lived up to the
tolerance of these words. It has pursued with fanatical vigour
those it considers devoid of ideological purity. One could
argue that the Baha'is — individually, rather than as a body —
should have distanced themselves from being associated with
the regime of the Shah. They might have known that their
success was causing jealousy, that their association with the
outside world was sure to be misconstrued in a xenophobic
country like Iran. It is a sad fact for them that they are now
suffering the jealous reaction of their despisers for having
failed to do this.

The economic success of the Baha'is under the regime of
the Shah is a major explanation then for the persecution
they have suffered under Khomeini. The charges laid against
them are in the main fictions created by their opponents to
cover an inveterate hatred. The Baha'i association with Israel,
as it emerges continually from 'trials' of Baha'is and from
government propaganda, has been wantonly distorted. Yet
this association, though one of an innocent and non-political
kind, is sufficient in itself to create in the minds of Shi'ites a

monstrous image of Zionist conspiracy.

The same factor lies behind the charge that Baha'is are agents of American imperialism. From the 1920s the presence of Americans in Iran was frequently attributed to them being either Baha'is themselves, or supporters of Baha'is. At one point an American diplomat was murdered by the mob in the belief he was a Baha'i. There was some justification for this view, though not for the act (the man concerned was not a Baha'i) for Baha'i missionary activity in the United States stretches back into the 1890s, when American pilgrims went to Palestine to see Abdu'l-Baha. From that time Baha'i successes in America were impressive, and the 1926 persecutions of Baha'is in Iran was met with activity on their behalf by American converts to the religion.

This association with the United States, like the economic success of some of their number, was an unfortunate qualification for the Baha'is to have in revolutionary, Islamic Iran. The activity of the American government in Iran during the period of the Shah was, to say the least, deeply resented by a large number of Iranians, probably with justification. The purchase of the Pepsi Cola franchise in Iran by Sabet further exacerbated the connection between the Baha'is and America in the eyes of the simple.

A curious example of how such a matter could raise religious passions is seen in the fatwa (clerical order) given by a mujtahid against the drinking of Pepsi Cola in the 1950s. This order according to M.J. Fischer was lately reaffirmed by Ayatollah Shariatmadari. Where the advance of Western technology met the thirteenth century religious mentality of the mujtahid, a curious state resulted. Yet the issue is axiomatic for understanding the causes of the Islamic Revolution, and its complete intolerance of the commercialism of the twentieth century. Islam forbade usury, and the Shah's Iran was built upon it, as western investors vied to gain a foothold in an Iranian economy giddy with the Shah's reckless injection of oil revenue in the 1970s. The Islamic conscience, and indeed the mass of the Iranian people, were not consulted on this question.

Yet the ugly face of capitalism was not how it had started

out. The Shah's 'White Revolution' begun in 1962 set out to modernise Iran, and in doing so he followed on the measures of his father, Reza Shah, offending Islamic conservatism by encouraging a more liberal social code, encouraging women to finally discard the veil and play their part in the modernisation of their country. The land reforms that gave the land to the peasantry, and the introduction of profit-sharing in industry to reconcile management and workers, both found endorsement in Baha'i teaching. Indeed, could the Shah have actually been reading Baha'i literature? Such an influence would be anathema to the hard-pressed clergy, but who really represented the way forward for the Iranian people? To reject the twentieth century it might not be possible to stop at Pepsi Cola. When the Shi'ite clergy formulated its demands on the Shah, they included: 'spread of Baha'ism, increasing numbers of Europeans in the administration, contracting of foreign loans . . .' as the evils to be fought.* To add to this, Baha'is appeared to adopt some of the Western ways so loathed by the mullas. They did not need the encouragement of Reza Shah to inspire their women to leave off the veil, and mix with the opposite sex in public. Neither were the Baha'is slow to adopt Western education. The antipathy between the mullas and the middle classes who espoused Western technology was particularly pointed in the case of the Baha'is, who achieved distinction in the modern modes of education that seemed to threaten the *madrasa* (religious seminary).

The other religious minorities were also suspect of course — the Christians could be expected to sympathise with the West, and the Zoroastrians were known to be patronised by the foreigner both in trade, and when it came to recruiting staff for diplomatic missions — Jews were automatically labelled Zionist. But the Baha'is were most hated, because in spite of their universalist belief, theologically the Iranian Baha'is remained conservative, close to many basic Shi'ih axioms. They not only accepted Muhammad and the Qur'an, they also endorsed the Shi'ih Imams, and Shit'ite view of the successorship to Muhammad. The similarities were intimate

* Fisher, op. cit., p. 185.

enough to make the divergencies abhorrent. The Baha'is maintained the twelfth Imam had returned in the person of the Bab, while proclaiming Baha'u'llah as the Promised One awaited by the entire human race. Such claims, if accepted, would mean the fulfilment of the Shi'ite prayer for the coming of the Imam, and would certainly obviate the need for the rôle filled by Ayatollah Khomeini (Nayib al-Imam, 'the deputy to the Imam' title adopted by Khomeini).

The most opprobrium that can be given a person in Khomeini's Iran is to call him a member or informer for SAVAK. This charge has accordingly been laid at the feet of Baha'is arrested by the Komitehs.

Parviz Sabeti, the powerful head of Military Intelligence section of SAVAK during the final years of the Shah's reign was popularly known as a Baha'i, with the same amount of justification the charge held for Hoveyda and Rouhani. Most of those Baha'is who received formal indictment before execution were accused of collaborating with SAVAK. Needless to say, they, their relatives, and their associates vehemently denied it. No evidence has been brought forward to substantiate such allegations; and where known SAVAK agents have been accredited with membership of the Baha'i Faith, Baha'i sources have likewise denied in the strongest terms that these figures were Baha'is. Baha'is are ready to point out, however, that their activities under the Shah were undoubtedly known about by the Shah's secret police, as they could hardly fail to have been. Whether the ranks of the Baha'is were ever penetrated by SAVAK agents, or whether Baha'i institutions voluntarily reported their activities to SAVAK, cannot be easily verified. The Baha'is maintain that they had nothing to hide at that time, as they do not have to hide anything from the present authorities.

Baha'i sources have countered these accusations by pointing to the activities of SAVAK against the Baha'is, which they say were spear-headed by the anti-Baha'i Islamic fanatics of the Tablighat-i-Islami organisation. According to these Baha'i sources, SAVAK and Talighat-i-Islami worked together over a period of years, harassing, propagandising, and actually inciting violence against the Baha'is. They give as an example the burning of Baha'i homes that occurred in the last month of 1978 — the last months also of the Shah's reign. To quote a Baha'i pamphlet: 'On 9 June [1980] one of the daily newspapers of Iran brazenly published a letter issued by the third bureau of SAVAK to its director, clearly indicating the connection between the Society and SAVAK. The letter carried the request of Tablighat-i-Islami for aid from SAVAK to attack the Baha'is in a scientific and logical way.'* The events that actually did occur in Shiraz and its environs in late 1978 are still disputed, both sides claiming aggression started with the other. The role of SAVAK at this period was certainly that of causing confusion with the intention of offsetting the growing revolutionary situation. Fereydoun Hoveyda, in his book, *The Fall of the Shah*, writes: 'The townspeople's [of Amol by the Caspian sea] imagination was haunted by the burning of the Rex cinema in Abadan, now definitely connected with SAVAK provocateurs. On 27 October there was a whisper that SAVAK was planning to set the bazaar on fire, and students and young people took to the streets armed with clubs in order to protect the population.' If SAVAK was bent on creating chaos at this time, what better diversion than a pogrom of Baha'is? Not only does it seem possible that Baha'i allegations are true, but given the desperation of the regime in autumn and winter of 1978, and its readiness, as recorded by Hoveyda, to throw to the wolves even longtime servants of the Shah like his brother, what scruples could SAVAK or even the Shah himself have had to sacrifice the Baha'is?

The difficulties of the Baha'is really began then with the death-throes of the Shah's regime. Well might they have had

---

* The newspaper was *Mujahid* — a Mujahidden paper opposed to Tablighat-i-Islami. That there was some complicity between the Muslim fundamentalists and SAVAK seems likely. However it should be remembered that these two organisations were themselves enemies of one another. The SAVAK reply also stipulates that Tablighat-i-Islami activities against the Baha'is must not 'be the cause of provocation and disturbance'.

cause to fear when they saw the approaching chaos, and remembered how fateful such times of turmoil had always been for them in the past. Those Baha'is who were rich and may have had reason to feel themselves compromised could make good their escape at this moment, when the writing was on the wall for the richer classes in Iran. The fact is that the vast majority of Baha'is remained, some no doubt because they had no alternative (like the simple countryfolk in the village of Nuk); others, like Dr. Samandari of Tabriz, because they would not shirk their responsibility. Having remained aloof from the agitation against the monarchy, the Baha'is had reason to fear reprisals from the victors who could be expected to accuse the Baha'is of sitting on the fence while their supporters had been dying in the streets.

It now required a different kind of heroism — an heroic passivity — to await the other face of the Islamic Revolution — its fanatical notion of justice — when your religious beliefs had kept you off the street in the first place, and you knew your refusal to join a popular revolution would be miscon-strued by the revolutionaries.

Though they had experienced fluctuating fortune under the previous regime, the Baha'is had remained loyal. In 1955 they were in a parlous position, and then above all their loyalty to the government was most severely tested. But the later years of Mohammed Reza Shah's reign were relatively tranquil for the Baha'is. It must be said that no Baha'i was imprisoned or executed for his belief under the Shah. Dis-crimination only existed on the lower level, in respect of the official refusal to recognise Baha'i marriage, and periodic dismissals of Baha'is from lesser Government posts.

Baha'is were no threat to the Shah, and enjoyed a period of relative tolerance, loosening their belts in this, for them, rare atmosphere. They knew well that no regime in Iran would go so far as to actually favour them, since they in return could never give active political support. And herein lay the precariousness of their position: when the Shah's regime began to choke and flay its arms in its death-throes, the Baha'is experienced the fickle nature of power, as SAVAK turned upon them and began the chain of persecution that has reached such fearful proportions under Ayatollah Khomeini. For even under the Shah, the clergy were the worst enemy of the Baha'is — now they were in power.

CHAPTER THREE

What Baha'is Believe

From the first years of the Babi Religion onwards, it has proved difficult for outsiders to focus very precisely on what the new Faith taught. The Bab's followers were accredited with pantheistic, nihilistic, communist beliefs, by Westerners in Persia. Despite accurate, sympathetic presentations of Babi-Baha'i teaching by the likes of Gobineau, Nicholas, Lord Curzon and E.G. Browne, similar problems have remained. What, for example, is the relationship between Baha'ism and Islam? We have already seen that there is a shared idiom among Baha'is and Shi'ites when it comes to theology, Baha'is following the Twelver sect of Islam in accepting the Imams and the notion of the occultation of the twelfth Imam, and his eventual return. Babis entered battle crying 'Ya Sahib-uz-Zahman!' — 'O Lord of the Age', thus bearing witness to the presence among them of the messiah of the Shi'ite Faith.

This closeness has caused Western writers one after the other to repeat the notion that the Baha'i Faith is a sect of Islam. Baha'is have, on the other hand, always rejected this, saying that their founders created a new Faith altogether, and further, they instance the separate scripture of the Baha'i Faith, its own laws, calendar, and its own holy places and pilgrimage. This evidence is persuasive, but has not been persuasive enough to make commentators forget the Islamic hinterland in which so much of the history of the new movement has take place. Baha'is also maintain — in contradistinction to the kind of categorising that puts them among reformist Islamic groups like the Pakistani Ahmadiyya and Sudanese

3 A famous Baha'i martyr awaits his execution in 1870.

5   The death of a Baha'i portrayed in a Persian magazine,
     1911.

Baha'is suffering for their religion: this father and son
await their execution, fastened together by a single
chain.

6 The Baha'i centre in Tehran before its destruction in 1955.

7 The Baha'i centre in Tehran after its destruction in 1955.

8   High-ranking officers in the Shah's army lend their arm
     to the demolishing of the Baha'i national headquarters,
     1955.

9   The Shi'ih preacher, Falsafi, looks on as the Baha'i
     headquarters in Tehran are demolished, 1955.

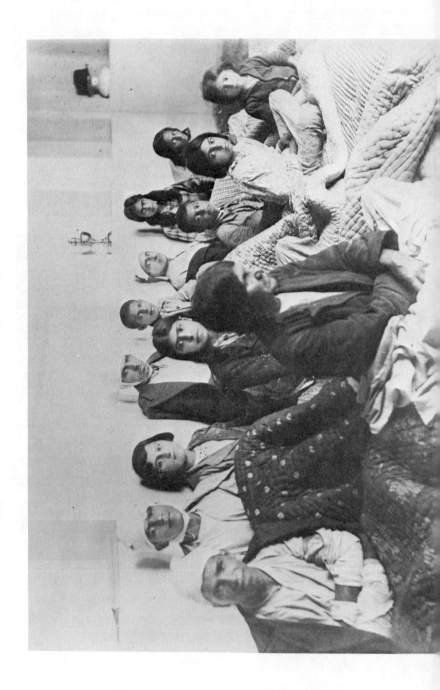

11   Desecrated Baha'i cemetery in Tehran, 1963.

10   Baha'is of peasant stock wounded during the upheavals
     in Abadih, 1955.

Mahdi-ists — that the point of reference in Baha'i teaching is no longer the Qur'an and the traditions of Islam. They see their own Faith as growing out of Islam into a new creation in the same way as Christianity grew out of Judaism. In his introduction to the standard Baha'i account of the first hundred years of their Faith, Shoghi Effendi wrote: 'I shall seek to represent . . . those momentous happenings which have . . . transformed a heterodox and seemingly negligible offshoot of the Shaykhi school of the Ithna-Ashariyyih sect of Shi'ah Islam into a world religion whose unnumbered followers are organically and indissolubly united . . .'*

The extent and scope of the modern-day Baha'i movement is pointed to with pride by the Baha'is, for they see in it the proof of the universalist pretensions of their religion. They often quote the words of Baha'u'llah that E.G. Browne recorded from his first interview with the great leader in Palestine in 1890:

> We desire but the good of the world and the happiness of the nations . . . That all nations should become one in faith and all men as brothers; that the bonds of affection and unity between the sons of men should be strengthened; that diversity of religion should cease, and the difference of race be annulled — what harm is there in this?

It is fair to say that this vision of the unity of mankind of their Faith's founder has remained at the centre of Baha'i belief and practice. Baha'is believe the message of unity enshrined in their religion has been the secret behind its remarkable growth from the Islamic Near East until it has spread through most areas of the globe. The argument that the majority of Baha'is now no longer come from Islamic backgrounds is supported by the recent successes among the Amerindians and East Indians. This transformation from a persecuted and proscribed sect of the Islamic world to a flourishing independent religious grouping in such various territories and among so many different races, must inevi-

* Shoghi Effendi, *God Passes By*, p. xii.

tably have radical implications for the development of Baha'i teaching. The Islamic ingredient in the emergence of Baha'ism has been both its blessing and its main limiting factor. The persecution suffered by Baha'is from Islamic backgrounds has undoubtedly given the Faith momentum, and as the present events in Iran show, has contributed to its emergence from obscurity and news value in the eyes of the world's media. Yet at the same time the Baha'is' association with the Islamic world has continued to hold the Baha'i Faith back in the minds of those intelligentsia who still consider it an offshoot of Islam. The Baha'is of Iran represent, there can be no doubt, the conservative side of Baha'ism, both culturally and theologically. Yet it must not be forgotten that it is due to their sacrifices, in the last century and at this moment, that the Baha'i Faith has achieved the wide dissemination it has done.

During the period when 'Abdu'l-Baha was head of the Baha'i Faith (1892-1921) missionaries were sent to North America, and they were followed by 'Abdu'l-Baha himself in 1912. Christian missionaries in Palestine had already met the Baha'i leader, known as 'the Master' to his followers, and had commented on his remarkable knowledge of the Bible and Church history. Some of them allowed this acknowledgement to turn into jealousy when they realized that 'Abdu'l-Baha's liberal interpretation of scripture and Christian doctrine was winning converts to the Baha'i Faith among Westerners. 'Abdu'l-Baha taught that there were two elements in religion: the social laws which were altered by the Prophets from dispensation to dispensation, and the essential spiritual truths which remained the same, above all the principle of love. The rational appeal of 'Abdu'l-Baha's exegesis of Christian dogmas and myths undoubtedly explained the interest educated Americans now took in the Baha'i Faith. This was all the more surprising when it is remembered that 'the Master' had received no formal education, having spent the bulk of his life in exile and even imprisonment in the company of his father.

The tolerance and rationality of the Baha'i teachings as interpreted by 'Abdu'l-Baha won praise from the likes of

Tolstoi and the Swiss social scientist, Auguste Forel, who called himself a Baha'i. Baha'is believe in the unity of the Prophets much as do Muslims, but the station of Christ is explained in terms that Christians could more easily accept, and the succession of messengers, or 'Manifestations of God', is held not to end with Muhammad, or even with Baha'u'llah. The aim of the successive appearance of these figures, among whom can be numbered Moses, Zoroaster, Buddha, Christ and Muhammad, is the progressive education of humanity. Civilization is ultimately built upon the teachings these Manifestations bring. The goal of religion in the modern age is to bring about the spiritual unity of the whole human race, to annul differences of creed and race as we saw in the extract from Browne. Among the teachings of the Baha'i Faith that fall into 'Abdu'l-Baha's social category are the principles which Baha'is say make their religion the one to answer the needs of modern man:

i. The oneness of mankind.
ii. The independent investigation of truth
iii. The common foundation of all religions.
iv. The essential harmony of religion and science.
v. Equality of men and women.
vi. Elimination of prejudices of all kinds.
vii. Universal compulsory education.
viii. A spiritual solution of the economic problem.
ix. A universal auxillary language.
x. Universal peace.

Numbers v, vii, viii, and ix clearly fall into the category of social teachings. Baha'is maintain that the equality of men and women is a wholly new principle to be found taught in a religion. The spiritual approach to economics is based upon the principle that excessive wealth and poverty should be abolished. Baha'ism does not preclude private enterprise or the charging of a moderate interest, but it is corporate in essence, and the interests of the community are held to be more important than those of the individual. Profit-sharing is enjoined, and a system of taxation that redistributes wealth more evenly throughout the community, as is seen in advanced countries today. However the creation of wealth can never be a goal in itself as it is in materialist societies now. 'Abdu'l-Baha's exposition of a future Baha'i society exphasizes the pre-eminence of agriculture, though technology is not spurned. The ideal community is a spiritually oriented one, linked to the world-wide community of small towns and nations, throughout the whole of which harmony is the most important aim.

This, to some, utopian vision holds out to humanity the hope of a time free from the animosities that afflict the world today. All force other than the token policing necessary for internal order will be eliminated — thus the great amount of wealth immorally squandered on armaments will be turned to the eradication of social evils like disease and poverty. The prerequisite for such a state of affairs is trust — Baha'is believe their vision is not utopian, but within the grasp of a spiritually developed race of mankind. This is why, they emphasize, the Baha'i teachings demand such a high ethical standard from the followers — they are to suffice for many generations to come, and under their shadow a new race of people must be raised up.

In order to facilitate the spread of trust and the breakdown of prejudice intermarriage between different races is highly praised. Individuals are also enjoined to broaden their outlook, for Baha'u'llah said: 'let your vision be all-embracing rather than confined to yourself'. Education is greatly valued, but not merely so that material advancement may be acquired. The obtaining of technical knowledge is necessary for gaining a livelihood, but the most important education is that which heightens the receptivity of the soul. The pursuit of the Arts is commended, for Art is fundamentally a spiritual activity, enriching perception and training the senses towards greater refinement.

Once the charge that the Baha'i Faith is a sect of Islam has been dropped, new ones arise. It has been classed in the category of the 'Frankenstein' approach to religion, where different elements are eclectically acquired and re-arranged in an artificial synthesis. This charge is from the opposite wing to the one which insists the Baha'i Faith is a sect of Islam; the thinking behind this one is that the Baha'i teachings are too progressive to emanate from a bona fide religious source, and so must have been put together by a committee somewhere. This charge is historically inept, and is usually made by sociologists. Examination of the texts on the one hand would prove the Baha'i teachings came from no other source than the two figures of Baha'u'llah and 'Abdu'l-Baha. Any investigation of the details of their lives would persuade the unbiased that they had no time to ransack the libraries of Palestine for all their progressive material.

However, it has to be admitted that the Baha'is themselves have not helped in the transmission of clear accounts of their Faith. The problem rests largely on the general ignorance among scholars and non-initiates of the facts of Baha'i history. Here, with the exception of Shoghi Effendi's rhetorical masterpiece, *God Passes By*, Baha'i historians are either far more partisan than is necessary, or turgid to the point of being unreadable.

It would also be too easily done to criticize the practice of the Baha'i Faith as it is found in its historically established centres in Iran, North America, and Europe. The believers in these areas tend to draw their numbers from the middle classes, and communities lack the dynamism and vitality of more popular centres like those to be found in Malaysia, India, and parts of Africa. Indeed the radical potential of Baha'i teachings on such matters as economics and the education of the masses must await the creation of a popular Baha'i state. The Baha'is in Iran might be accused of quietism within their own country, yet Iranians have never realized the extent to which the Baha'i Faith has grown outside of Iran itself, mainly as a result of the pioneering efforts of Iran's Baha'is. Also, on inter-racial harmony and instituting of equal rights for women, the Baha'i communities have often produced progressive results, revealing again the potential of Baha'ism.

Where the Baha'is make a practical contribution to the development of world consciousness through the teachings of their Faith is in the fields of United Nations organisations and inter-Faith movements. At the United Nations the Baha'is have non-political consultative status, and are represented by a permanent staff called the International Baha'i Community. The Baha'i point of view is frequently presented at conferences and seminars on world problems. To the United Nations Commission on the Status of Women, the International Baha'i Community tendered the following, which is an extract from item 3, 11 January 1974 session:

> To encourage the independent search for truth, free of influence of family, community or nation. This is not to say that women are to be taught *a* truth, but rather that the spirit of free, impartial and independent investigation should lead in a constructive way to the breaking of inhibiting and outmoded traditional patterns and lead ultimately to unity of understanding and of action. The spirit of independent thought must be fostered if women are to gain knowledge, conviction and courage to take initiative in abandoning traditional ways which impede not only their own advancement but the advancement of men as well.
> 3. To stress that the principle of equality in rights does not necessarily imply that men and women should, or must, exercise the same functions. There are differences between men and women in qualities and powers: mental alertness, intuition and the spiritual qualities of love and service are qualities in which women are strong. There is need for greater emphasis on these qualities and a better balance between spiritual and material powers if humanity is to progress. However, 'the fact that there is no equality in functions between the sexes should not infer that either sex is inherently superior or inferior to the other, or that they are unequal in their rights'. (From the Baha'i writings.)

The following is part of a statement given by the Baha'i representative at the United Nations Conference on World Population, Bucharest, on 19 August, 1974:

> This conviction by the individual and society of the essential unity of the human race is the only viable standard today for social and economic justice. On it must depend the successful solution of the population

problem — as of the problems of environment, poverty, disease, unemployment, etc. 'It means briefly to consider the welfare of the community as one's own . . . to regard humanity as a single individual, and one's own self as a member of that corporeal form, and to know of a certainty that if pain or injury afflicts any member of that body, it must inevitably result in suffering for all the rest.' (Baha'i writings).

At the local level as well, Baha'is have become consistent supporters of the United Nations Associations.

Believing in the essential oneness of religion, the contribution of the Baha'is in fostering religious understanding among the different Faiths of mankind has been good. This is somewhat ironic when Baha'is themselves have been so often the victim of discrimination and persecution on the grounds of their beliefs — or perhaps it is because of this that they have retained such tolerance. In Britain the Baha'is are affiliated to the World Federalists, and are frequently to be found organising and participating in inter-Faith services. Baha'is have also been active for many years in the World Congress of Faiths organisation, founded by Francis Younghusband.

Most observers on the Baha'i Faith without an axe to grind have recognised it as a force for good, devoid of ulterior aim or political pretension. While Baha'i resources are not great enough as yet to enter into philanthropic work on a grand scale, the social consciousness of the religion accounts for the high proportion of doctors, nurses, teachers, and related occupations within the ranks of the Baha'is. Among the admirers of the young religion was Arnold Toynbee, and he summarises succinctly the status of the Baha'i Faith:

> My opinion is that (i) Bahaism is undoubtedly a religion, (ii) Bahaism is an independent religion on a par with Islam, Christianity and the other recognised world religions. Bahaism is not a sect of some other religion; it is a separate religion and it has the same status as the other recognised religions. This opinion is based both on study and on personal acquaintance with Baha'is.

On receipt of a tablet sent to her by Baha'u'llah in 1870,

Queen Victoria is reputed to have said: 'if this be of God it will endure; if not, no ill can come of it'. Many people who have had acquaintance with the Baha'is, and their peace-loving ways, are dismayed by the fact that such a harmless creed should attract such hatred, distortion of its teachings, and loss of life among its members, from the hands of its inveterate enemies in the land of its birth.

It is probably true to say that the impact of this new religion has yet to make itself really felt; that it looks more to a future, than to the present or to the past. The guardianship of such a future rests with the world governing body of the Baha'is, The Universal House of Justice. Ordained by the Prophet-Founder of the religion, this body of nine men looks over the progress of the Faith, and protects it from schism or sectarianism. The wide range of backgrounds from which Baha'is are drawn ensures a great latitude of cultural opinion within the Baha'i Faith; the world governing body claims the allegiance and obedience of all believers and is a potent force for the future cohesion of the movement.

The election of local and national governing institutions protects the democratic franchise of the mass of believers, but members of these bodies are held to be responsible only to their consciences and to the divinity. These elections are annual, in the case of The Universal House of Justice, every five years. No electioneering is practised or accepted; personality and careerism are frowned upon. A process of consultation is the norm within Baha'i communities, and decisions are collectively reached, never autocratically. Baha'i institutions have the power to discipline believers by removing their credentials, or expelling them outright. Power is therefore both diffuse and centralised; a substantial local autonomy is envisaged for the individual, local community. It is here that Baha'is look for the government of the future. This presents an exciting prospect to the detached observer, because here it seems the Baha'is have a lot to give to the rest of mankind, struggling as it is at the moment between the diverse pulls of centralisation and the demand for smaller units of decision making. The Baha'is go even further and write into their constitution a special clause for the protection of minority

interests. Previously oppressed minorities within conglomer-
ate states find the Baha'i Faith attractive for this reason, and
Baha'is for their part seem particularly anxious to enrol
indigenous racial and religious minorities.

The Baha'is look to this system of government — which
can seem complicated at first view, but rests on the principles
of democratic, consultative, collective decision-making — as
the pattern of a future world order. They see the present
systems in operation in the world as doomed to failure, and
adhere so strictly to their own institutions and procedure
that it could easily be said that these are nine-tenths of their
religion.

However, it is also true to say that the Baha'i religion
contains devotional and mystic ingredients. The rationalism
of 'Abdu'l-Baha, for example, is enhanced by a subtle mysti-
cism which at first sight appears to draw from the classic Sufi
tradition. The love and devotion which the believer feels
toward God and expresses in the Sufi tradition by adherence
to a perfect master, in the Baha'i Faith is channelled through
the figures of the Bab and Baha'u'llah. However these are
not worshipped as personalities, but held rather to be perfect reflections of the Divinity. Indeed, the eminence of
Baha'u'llah is felt to be so great by some that they turn to
'Abdu'l-Baha as a perfect reflection in turn of the Manifestation's light. Like the Sufis, Baha'is have strong veneration
for past repositories of the Word of God, holding Moses,
Jesus and Muhammad on the same level of admiration. But
this turning to centres of light does not mean that religious
law is overlooked — in legalistic religions the law is held to no
more firmly than among the Baha'is.

The terminology of Baha'i devotionalism is again akin to
the mystic traditions: the purpose of man's existence is to
know and love his creator. This can be expressed in more
abstract terms as the journey of the soul toward God. As in
the Hindu and Sufi traditions, the Baha'i writings place great
emphasis upon dissolution of the single self in the Divine
Self; the individual soul is possessed of attributes of divinity
were it only to cleanse itself of the dross of its mundane
existence. The Baha'i teachings maintain however that the

individual is immeasurably weaker than God himself, and to suggest any equality between creator and created is a fundamental error.

This mixture of traditionalism and innovation is held by Baha'is to be as it should, for new social teachings are coupled with the eternal verities in any new religious revelation. To Baha'is 'Revelation' is a key word: they see their Faith as the conscious creation of divinity rather than an effort by man to reach God. Baha'u'llah is not God in essence — to suggest such a thing would seem to them both absurd and faintly blasphemous, since God is unknowable, beyond egress and regress — he is however a being set apart, more than ordinary man could ever be, but less than God. He is a divine manifestation, a separate creation, yet at the same time born of the World of God which is uncreated and eternal.

To expand on Toynbee's remarks on the status of the Baha'i Faith, there can be no doubt that in time it will make a remarkable contribution to the spiritual and intellectual consciousness of mankind, enriching its day to day life, and inspiring its hopes, as the other great religions have done in the past. The present sufferings of the Iranian Baha'is have to be seen in context: the unfolding of a new system of religious belief that must add its contribution to the spiritual development of the human race as a whole. These are but the early days of the religion, and each religion involves its followers in trials and sufferings when it first appears in the world.

The Baha'i Faith — A Chronology

1844	Beginning of the Babi movement.
1850 9 July	Execution of the Bab in Tabriz on orders of Mirza Taqi Khan, Amir-Nizam (Prime Minister).
1852	Attempt on life of Shah by three Babis; thousands of Babis massacred on orders of Shah Nasiri'd-Din.
1853	Exile of Baha'u'llah to Baghdad.

1863 21 April	Baha'u'llah declares himself to be the 'Promised One' foretold by the Bab. He subsequently leaves Iraq for further exile in Turkey, spending three months in the Ottoman capital, Constantinople.
1863-68	Further exile in Adrianople, and in August 1868, banishment to the penal colony of Acre (Akka) in Palestine.
1868-70	Baha'u'llah and his family and some supporters spend two years in the citadel-prison in Acre.
1879	Baha'u'llah moves from town of Acre to comfortable lodging in surrounding countryside. The last decade of his life is spent in the mansion of Bahji, where he is alone except for family and close supporters. Edward Granville Browne, an exception, is allowed an audience in spring 1890.
1892	Death of Baha'u'llah. Leadership of the Baha'i community devolves upon 'Abdu'l-Baha, Baha'u'llah's eldest son and appointed successor.
1893	The Baha'i Faith is mentioned by a Protestant missionary to Persia at the World Congress of Religions in Chicago.
	The Baha'i Faith gains footing in the United States. Opens the way for the beginning of Baha'i groups in Europe.
1911-13	'Abdu'l-Baha visits Europe twice, en route and returning from America.
1921	Death of 'Abdu'l-Baha. His grandson, Shoghi Effendi Rabbani, appointed as 'Guardian' of the Baha'i Cause by 'Abdu'l-Baha's will.
1920s	Establishment of National Assemblies of the Baha'is in Britain, India, the United States, Germany, and Egypt.

1925	Muslim court in Egypt pronounces the Baha'i Faith an independent religion, not a sect of Islam.
1940s and 1950s	World-wide spread of the Baha'i Faith enhanced by plans of teaching inaugurated by Shoghi Effendi. The 'Ten Year Crusade' is only four years old when he dies in 1957.
1963	Crusade carried on to 1963, when The Universal House of Justice is elected and holds its first meeting in London.
1970	Over 100,000 Baha'i centres in the world. Baha'i community has consultative status with UN ECOSOC, and subsequently (1976) with UNICEF.

CHAPTER FOUR

Destroying the Defenceless

The Persecution of the Baha'is:
1. February 1979 to September 1980

The gathering forces that were to overthrow the Shah of Iran encompassed the deaths of thousands of people. Unnoticed in that unheaval were the deaths of a few Baha'is, murdered by pillaging mobs in outlying areas of the country. Some now see the hand of SAVAK behind the killing of a father and son in Miyan-Du'ab in December 1978, or the burning to death of two Baha'is in Shahmirzad, that August. The Baha'is in the Shiraz area were particularly hard-pressed, but this was to be only the beginning.

The first real act of aggression against the Baha'is that connected a ready nerve was the sacking and demolition of the House of the Bab in Shiraz, so often in the past the object of anti-Baha'i vengeance. This exquisite building was seized by a mob of some twenty or more assailants, led by a local mulla. Later to be represented as a wayward act of an uncontrolled group of vandals, this seizure resulted in the entire razing to the ground of the holy property. Baha'is maintain that this shameful act, which occurred in September 1979, was perpetrated by twenty-five revolutionary guardsmen, accompanied by the head of religious endowments department in Shiraz. The systematic way in which the building was demolished is shown in photographs secretly taken whilst the destruction was going on. Later, plans to construct a road through the middle of the site were announced by the authorities, and the occupants of adjacent houses, mostly owned by Baha'is, were instructed to vacate their properties.

Photographs of the ruins of the House of the Bab reveal

anti-Baha'i grafitti; similar inscriptions were to be found on the graves of Baha'is that began to be desecrated. The attacks on Baha'i cemeteries and holy places could perhaps be construed as the acts of 'unruly mobs'; the forced abductions and demands placed upon Baha'is to renounce their faith were another matter. They involved the complicity of the clergy of the mosques to which the Baha'is were taken. But the seizure of the assets of the Baha'i Community, and the dismissal of Baha'is from their posts in the civil service denoted a measure of official involvement in the campaign against Baha'is that it was hard to deny.

Indeed, what could be the point in denial anyway? The leaders of the Islamic Revolution doubtless had as their first concern the settling of their scores with the agents of the old regime. But the clerical element that was soon to gain so powerful a hold upon the government of Iran made no secret of its distaste for the Baha'is. A spokesman for Ayatollah Khomeini in Washington, interviewed in the first days of the new regime, is reported to have told a leading member of the American Jewish community that the rights of Iranian Jews would be respected:

> However, Mr. Gold reported, Mr. Rouhani said that the 200,000 to 300,000 members of the Bahai faith, which the Ayatollah is said to regard as a political rather than a religious movement, would not receive the same guarantees.
>
> (*New York Times*, 14 February 1979)

This same message could be gleaned from an interview published in the American magazine, *Seven Days*, in which the Ayatollah Khomeini, then an exile in Paris, answered questions put to him on the kind of regime he would lead if brought to power in Iran. He undertook at first to recognise and protect all religious minorities, but when specifically asked: 'Will there be either religious or political freedom for the Baha'is under an Islamic government', he replied: 'They are a political faction; they are harmful; they will not be accepted'. Asked if Baha'is would be allowed freedom of practice for their religion, he answered 'No'. (*Seven Days*,

23 February 1979). Khomeini represents the mainstream Shi'ite disapproval of the Baha'i Faith as something known to be bad, or 'harmful'. His prejudices only needed to be fuelled, and to perform this task there existed two specifically anti-Baha'i, fanatically Shi'ite factions.

One, as we have seen, is the Tablighat-i-Islami, formed in the 1960s with the expressed purpose of attacking the Baha'is, an intent which they fulfilled countless times in frequenting Baha'i meetings and attempting to break them up. Baha'is sometimes responded by evicting these people from the meeting themselves, and this reinforced the anti-Baha'i hatred of this faction. Tablighat-i-Islami was able thus to function under the Shah. although their own orientation was decidedly against the Pahlavi regime. Indeed, it is suggested that the Tablighat-i-Islami faction used its anti-Baha'i activities as a cloak for its more fundamental purpose — that of fighting the Shah. A leading member, one Shaykh Hallabi, (said to be the head of the organisation) has been able to set himself up as an expert on the Baha'is, and has provided the regime with its main propaganda plank against the Baha'is — namely, that they are Zionist. Khomeini's statements about Jews whilst he was in exile reveal a bias against them, and an association of those in Iran with Israel and the United States, that hardly accords with the guarantee of tolerance reported in the *New York Times* in February 1979. As the early months of the Islamic regime saw particularly virulent anti-American, anti-Zionist pronouncements and activities (culminating in the taking of the American hostages) — so it can be appreciated how potent the charge of collaboration with the forces of Zionism and American Imperialism might be when applied to Baha'is. The charge was wholly opportunist, but none the less effective.

A second anti-Baha'i group, perhaps even more violent in its hatred than Tablighat-i-Islami, is the Fada'iyan-i-Islam. This group openly claimed responsibility for the murder of a Baha'i doctor in Kashan, some years ago. Their report appeared in the newspaper, *Bamdad*, on 23 February 1980. A recent nominee for the premiership, 'Ali-Akbar Vellayati, rejected by the Majlis, probably on the grounds he was too extreme, was a member of Fada'iyan-i-Islam. Baha'i sources maintain that this group is now the most active force against them in Iran.

After the violence against the Baba'is in the neighbourhood of Shiraz immediately before the return of Khomeini to Iran, there followed a short period during which the fate of the Baha'is was held in abeyance. The occupation of Baha'i centres and holy places that began soon after was done according to the authorities, for the sake of their 'protection'. Representatives of the new Government did however meet with several members of the Baha'i National Assembly, and indeed contacts between the two were not at once founded upon hostility. But the extreme elements within the Government coalition were already gaining the upper hand, and Baha'is could only expect the worse from their victory. Moreover, in the chaotic conditions that pervaded Iran as a whole, much depended upon the activities of local 'Komitehs' — and their composition was of vital importance, for where dominated by the enemies of the Baha'is, their reign against local communities and individuals could not be gainsaid. Baha'i meetings were interrupted, and the speakers taken and questioned. Files and papers were taken from Baha'i centres. Baha'i institutions responded by contacting various authorities in Iran, trying to inform them of the true character of their faith. Pamphlets and covering letters were sent to powerful people in the regime.

It was to be only after failures in efforts to change government policy towards the Baha'is from inside Iran, that Baha'is outside Iran began mobilising international opinion.

The systematic order in which Baha'i premises were raided shortly after the establishment of the Khomeini regime in February 1979 has led to speculation as to whether as early as then, important elements within the new order were planning to extirpate the Baha'i Faith from Iran. The documents seized in the headquarters of the National Assembly of the Baha'is in Tehran included a list of the names of the entire Baha'i membership, as well as those who were most prominent in the community. This attack was repeated in a number of other Baha'i centres in the country. Needless to say, with these lists in the hands of the authorities, Baha'is throughout Iran have entertained considerable trepidation about their ultimate future from that time onwards. In Tehran itself, Baha'is received a letter from an outside source in August 1979, thus demonstrating the knowledge of the Baha'i membership list on the part of the sender.

The position of the Baha'i Community in Iran in September 1979 was summarised in a confidential report prepared by The Federation of Protestant Churches in Switzerland. Human Rights Commission. This completely independent report is worth quoting from extensively because of its third party status, and reliability and accuracy.

(English translation from the original German.)

'The Baha'i Community in Iran has a tradition and history in this country dating back to 1844. During the ensuing years, members of the Community have contributed to the education and welfare of the Iranian nation and have been loyal citizens and peace-loving individuals. They . . . support the religious proposition that Baha'i believers may *not* participate in any political movement in Iran. [Reference is then made to the refusal of the Baha'is to join the Shah's Rastakhiz Party.]

'Recently a national referendum was held on the question of whether to form an Islamic Republic in Iran or not. The ballot had two possible answers: Yes or No. The Baha'i national leadership wrote to Prime Minister Bazargan and said that their religious convictions would not allow any Baha'i to vote in the national referendum. Such a written statement issued during the tense days of the post-revolution fervour again exhibited the amazing courage of their convictions.

'The report that follows is a collection of facts gathered by the author and presented in the belief that religious harassment of the Baha'is and their faith has reached proportions which call for a concerted effort by non-aligned nations and third world media to publicize this state of affairs with the purpose of preventing further loss of property and possible loss of life to the 450,000 members of this Community here.

[The author then says he intends to treat his subject under the heads of administration, financial, personal and social persecution of Baha'is. Under the category, *Administrative Strangulation*, he details the occupation of Baha'i Centres and seizure of membership lists and files, already referred to.]

'Places attacked include the headquarters of the National Spiritual Assembly, the Tehran Spiritual Assembly Center and the Baha'i District Committees' Coordinating Center of Tehran. The City youth center for Baha'i young people was occupied. Efforts were made to move the Tehran Spiritual Assembly to another area. This was done several times and on each occasion the new premises were attacked shortly after they started up work again.

'Spiritual meetings and religious classes while in session suffered the same fate. Revolutionary militiamen would invade the premises of these gatherings and break them up. They acted on the excuse that reports of anti-revolutionary activities were taking place. Often the religious teachers were arrested and taken away and held several hours. On one occasion a teacher was held for several days. They were interrogated, frightened and placed under heavy psychological stress. When released, these leaders and teachers had to sign a statement pledging not to attend or promote "unauthorized or anti-revolutionary meetings".

[The mailing of letters to Baha'is in Tehran by an outside organization is mentioned next. The author assumed those responsible were part of the Tablighat-i-Islami. He concludes the section by comparing the size of the Baha'is to the other religious minorities in Iran.]

2 — Financial Strangulation

'The Baha'is of Iran have formed a commercial company called the Sharkat Umana (the Trustees' Company). In early June a letter from the Bunyad Mustaz'a'fan (The Foundation for the Dispossessed) directed an employee of this organization to take whatever action necessary in determining the identification and verification of the place and purpose of the Sharkat Umana. The reason for this directive was that the Sharkat Umana had been officially confiscated by the direct order of the National Iranian Islamic Public Prosecutor's Office.

'Under the Islamic system of government [i.e. as practised in Iran] the phrase "confiscated properties" connotes those properties which belonged to criminals in Iran executed for crimes against humanity and corruption on earth OR whose leaders stand accused of usury.

'A sub-section of the "Foundation For The Dispossessed" is called "The Department of Confiscated Properties" and it is this sub-section which officially took over the Sharkat Umana.

'When the offices of the Sharkat Umana were occupied by representatives of the Foundation, all employees were called together into one large room. One by one each was interrogated in front of the whole group. They were accused of being guilty of the following:

— Baha'is are agents of Zionism
— Baha'is are collaborators with Israel
— Baha'is have been identified as composing over half the known staff of torturers in SAVAK
— Baha'is lived under the protection of SAVAK

'The manager of the company was ordered to hand over the keys to all strong boxes, safes and locked files. Then he was commanded to appoint a person to take representatives of the Foundation to each piece of property that is owned by the Sharkat Umana. This person is now being forced to show all the Baha'i properties (one by one) to the Foundation representative. This investigation is being carried out based on the ownership documents found in the Sharkat Umana.

'All assets and furnishings of the Company were taken over by these men from the Foundation. All employees of the Company were summarily dismissed on that day and told not to come back to work for any reason.

'The sobering meaning of this act is that all income producing property plus buildings and land used solely for Baha'i

religious purposes are being taken over by the Islamic government of Iran.

[The report then proceeds to name some of the properties
seized, including the National Baha'i Headquarters, Baha'i
cemeteries, and the Baha'i-run hospital in Tehran. The
following details are then given of the taking over of the
Nawnahalan Company.]

Sharkat Nawnahalan (The Children's Company)

'This investment company was taken over in early June by
representatives of the Foundation.

'This company is a completely Baha'i owned organization.
It was founded in 1917 as a company to encourage Baha'i
children to begin life by being thrifty and saving a little of
their allowances each month for the future. This company
got its name from this programme.

[The report then mentions the assets of the company, the
number of shareholders — who it is noted are overwhelmingly
Baha'is — and the division of company capital.]

'Fifty percent of the equity of this company is held by the
Baha'i Community (this includes many of the local Baha'i
assemblies in cities and villages over Iran . . .). The other fifty
per cent is held by individual shareholders who are mostly
Baha'i children or [adults] who started saving there as a
child and now . . . continue with the plan.

'The importance of this company for the Baha'is is two-
fold:

1. It is one of the main financial centers for the Baha'i
Community in Iran. With the confiscation of this company the work of the Baha'i Community over Iran will be
paralyzed.

2. Because most of the shareholders and depositors of this
company are Baha'is and many have put most — if not all —
their savings for the future into this organization, the personal loss to thousands of Baha'is is incalculable.

'When this company was taken over, the revolutionary
guards told the officials that it was being confiscated because
it was anti-Islamic and was participating in the field of

financial credit which rightly only belongs to recognized and registered banks in Iran. Also it was said that the company was guilty of collecting funds in the form of usury.

'Although the company has been taken over, all shares are still in circulation and the representatives of the Foundation are saying that they will continue to be so until such time as the Central Committee of the Foundation decides on the best use of the company's assets and profits.

'If the present progression of events continues it is anticipated that with the confiscation of these facilities by the Islamic authorities, the Baha'i Community in Iran will be deprived of every vestige of property all over the nation.

3 — Social and Personal Strangulation

'It is estimated that there are now about twenty Baha'is in Qasr Prison Tehran [September 1979]. It is believed that all these Baha'is were arrested on trumped up charges, all of which omitted any reference to their being Baha'i. The pretext being used against these Baha'is in prison includes the following:
   — being a former senior Iranian military officer
   — being a large landowner
   — being an extraordinarily wealthy person
   — being a former high-ranking civil servant

'There is also personal economic repression. A businessman was arrested in the middle of the night and was later released after he had "volunteered to contribute" two million rials (thirty thousand US dollars) to the Revolutionary Central Committee. As far as is known, none of the three hundred plus men executed under the Islamic Revolutionary Regime has been a Baha'i. [The first Baha'i to be 'judicially' executed was Bahar Vujdani on 17 September 1979; the next, Azamatu'llah Fahandizh, on 14 December 1979 — the first in Mahabad, the second in Shiraz. The floodgates opened with the execution of three Baha'is in Tehran in May 1980.]

'Photocopies of letters of termination of employment from Iranian Government agencies are on file with Baha'i officials in Tehran showing clearly that at least fifty Baha'is

— men and women — have been openly dismissed from government service since the revolution because they are believers in the Baha'i Faith. Letters of complaint have been sent to Imam Khomeini and the Prime Minister's Office but these have not even been acknowledged.

'A leading Moslem Ayatollah has stated that Baha'is are people whom Moslems may annihilate without fear of punishment.

[The report then mentions areas where Baha'is have been forcibly made to recant their faith.]

'The proposed constitution of Iran does not recognize the Baha'i Faith as a legitimate religious body in the New Islamic Republic. They will have no rights of personal status if it is approved. This means that they must deny their faith in order to get married, divorced, distribute inheritances and estates and in adopting children because they must pretend to be somebody else to do these acts. The reason? These four acts of personal status are religious acts which must be done according to the rules of one of the four recognized religions of the country — of which the Baha'i Faith is not ... [one].

'Some religious leaders of the Islamic Faith have been asked why the Baha'is were not mentioned in the proposed constitution. One answer has been that since there are so few Baha'is in the country it is useless to designate [the Baha'is] as legitimate [because they are] such an insignificant minority. This is said about the *largest* of the four religious minorities in Iran!

'Some conservative and fanatical Moslem leaders call Baha'is apostates because Baha'is believe that Baha'u'llah represents a manifestation of God after the Prophet Mohammed. A minority of Moslems accuse Baha'is of saying that the Hidden Imam — Mehdi — has returned in the form of the Bab. In this ... context an Ayatollah has announced that on the 15th of Sha'aban (July 10, 1979, which is the birthday of the 12th or Hidden Imam of Shi'ite Islam) he will personally celebrate the birthday of Mehdi in the Hazirat'ul-Quds [Baha'i Centre] ... in Shiraz and would exhibit contempt ... for the Baha'i Faith [by this action].

'Several weeks ago in Mashad two of the leading

Ayatollahs announced with great fanfare that twenty-five Baha'i centers had been discovered in that city and were raided and "cleansed" by revolutionary guards. In reality, the "twenty-five" centers included two Baha'i centers and twenty-three homes of prominent members of the Baha'i community in Mashad. The homes have been returned to their owners but the two centers have been turned into Islamic study organizations. Why were these Baha'i facilities in Mashad raided? The newspaper wrote that Baha'is are "spies for the USSR, the USA, the UK and Israel"!

'There is fear based on the confiscation of Baha'i property and funds that the next logical step will be further to openly and aggressively seek the involuntary conversion of the Baha'is to Islam.'

The Baha'i International Community at the United Nations in New York has published its own account of the situation of the Baha'i Community in Iran, entitled: *The Baha'is in Iran: A Report on the Persecution of a Religious Minority* (June 1981). A more up-to-date rendering of the persecution, it lists what it sees as the aims of the Iranian Government vis-à-vis the Baha'i minority:

> Responsible government officials in Iran have inadvertently confirmed in private conversations that such a plan [i.e. to obliterate the Baha'is from Iran] exists and that the eradication of the Baha'i community is to be accomplished by the following means:
> — the arrest and execution of prominent Baha'is
> — the confiscation of the assets of the Baha'i community
> — the financial strangulation and intimidation of individual Baha'is to force them to recant their Faith.

The Swiss account illustrates how the first actions of the regime in Iran were to carry out the second and third aims — the confiscation of the assets of the Baha'i Community (the Umana and Nawnahalan companies — effectively Baha'i cooperatives); and the financial strangulation and intimidation of individual Baha'is to force them to recant their faith. The dismissal of Baha'is from their employment and the with-holding of their pensions and salaries had barely got underway in September 1979. Documents from official sources dismissing Baha'is and forbidding payment of monies to them are reproduced below — here, we can quote from several. As soon as the Islamic Republic was founded, the Ministry of Education, then under the direction of Mohammed Ali Rahai, announced plans for a full-scale purge of all Baha'i teachers. The pro-Government newspaper, *Etela'at*, on February 18, 1980, confirmed that this process was going forward by quoting the Director of Education in Azarbaijan province. According to the newspaper, the Director, Dr. Nayyrivand, said:

> During this week 30 persons employed in the Department of Education in this province who have collaborated with SAVAK and 50 who are Baha'is have been dismissed from their jobs. ... if the Baha'is accept Islam, they will again be employed and can return to their former jobs; otherwise, their files will be sent to the Revolutionary Courts in Tabriz for investigation.

In late October 1979, Rajai himself wrote a circular from the Ministry of Education in which he stated: 'the Ministry of Education ... cannot tolerate, like the previous regime, the existence of the followers of the Baha'i sect in its Educational unit, and in this way defile and deviate the minds and thoughts of innocent students. ... I would remind you that employment of Iranians who are not followers of recognized religions, such as Muslims, Jews, Christians and Zoroastrians, in Government Offices is against the law.'

Not only were Baha'i teachers dismissed, Baha'i students began to experience discrimination on the same grounds: that they were not able to state on college forms that they were of one of the four recognized religions. Later, this implicit discrimination against Baha'i students became explicit when the Government introduced its registration laws designed to isolate the Baha'i Community entirely.

Baha'i doctors and social workers increasingly suffered dismissal during 1980; retired army officers lost their pensions, and prominent Baha'i professors and lecturers were dispensed with.

By mid-1980, the Baha'i Community in Iran was therefore stripped of its collective assets, denied all legal recognition and thus placed outside the protection of the law, and its individual members were suffering every kind of discrimination and harassment. While the evidence of government representatives' remarks made it quite obvious that Baha'is were being persecuted because they were Baha'is, the Government still maintained that human rights of all groups were being respected in Iran. At this point, discrimination of Baha'is was semi-official — everyone knew it operated, but the pretence mentioned in the Swiss report that Baha'is were not suffering for their religion, but because of the 'crimes' they committed under the previous regime, had not been entirely removed.

Such executions as there had been by early 1980, if they involved Baha'is were ascribed to the perfunctory charges of Zionism, supporting SAVAK, promoting prostitution, and 'corruption on earth'. However, by the summer the authorities clearly entered on the most heinous part of their programme against the Baha'is: they began to execute prominent Baha'is in groups, and they no longer omitted to charge them with promoting the Baha'i Faith. At this juncture, Baha'is outside Iran, who had from the beginning been lobbying opinion in their own countries and making representations to Iranian embassies and consulates abroad, now feared their worst premonitions were in the process of coming true. At this moment too, the world's media began to speak of the darkness hanging over the Baha'is in Iran. 'What makes the new wave of persecutions so alarming,' said *The Times* on 15 July 1980, 'is that courts are beginning to prosecute, and even legitimize executions, on the ground that the accused person is a Baha'i.'

In a formal statement issued on September 15, the European Parliament declared that the Iranian Baha'i Community was the object of 'a systematic campaign of persecution', listed the three main fronts on which the campaign was being conducted, and called upon the Iranian Government to grant the Baha'is their protection and freedom to practise their religion. Appeals came from Amnesty International representatives, and from the Archbishop of Canterbury. The Iranian Government, still in the middle of the debate surrounding the holding of American hostages after the sack of the United States Embassy in Tehran, and on the verge of a war with Iraq, made no response.

These stark facts threw into dark relief the silence of the Iranian authorities:

6 May 1980	— Ghulam-Husayn A'azami, Badi'u'llah Yazdani, 'Ali-Akbar Mu'ini EXECUTED IN TEHRAN
11 May 1980	— Parviz Bayani EXECUTED IN PIRAN-SHAHR
3-16 June	— Muhajmad-Rida Hisami, Qudsiyyih Vahdat, Inayatul'llah Mihdizadih IMPRISONED IN SHIRAZ
5 June-19 July	— 'Abdu'l-'Ali Asadyari, Husayn Asadullahzadih, Ishmail Zihtab, Perviz Firuzi IMPRISONED IN TABRIZ
17 June	— Habibu'llah 'Azizi IMPRISONED IN TEHRAN (LATER EXECUTED)
27 June	— Yusif Subhani EXECUTED IN TEHRAN
14 July	— Faramarz Samandari, Yadu'llah Astani EXECUTED IN TABRIZ
16 July	— 'Ali Dadash-Akbari EXECUTED IN RASHT
30 July	— Yadu'llah Mahbubiyan EXECUTED IN TEHRAN
15 August	— Dhabihu'llah Mu'mini EXECUTED IN TEHRAN
21 August	— Abdu'l-Husayn Taslimi, Hushang Mahmudi, Ibraham Rahmani, Husayn Naji, Manuhir Qa'im Maqami,

'Ata'u'llah Muqarribi, Yusif Qadimi, Mrs. Bahiyyih Nadiri, Kambiz Sadiqzadih, Yusif 'Abbasiyan, Hishmat'u'llah Rawhani EIGHT PROMINENT BAHA'IS INCLUDING NINE MEMBERS BAHA'I NATIONAL ASSEMBLY ARRESTED, WHEREABOUTS NOW UNKNOWN

8 September — Nuru'llah Akhtarkhavari, Mahmud Hasanzadih, 'Azizu'llah Dhabihiyan, Firaydun Faridani, 'Abdu'l-Vahab Kazimi Manshadi, Jalal Mustaqim, Ali Mutabhari EXECUTED IN YAZD

In the battle for the minds of the world's public opinion, the Islamic Republican regime in Iran has had little success, either in respect of its behaviour toward internal minorities such as Kurds, Jews, Christians, or Baha'is; or in respect of the ideological face it has turned to the outside world. It is clear that the Iranian Government has been surprised by the adverse press it has received on the subject of its persecution of the Baha'i Faith.

The position of the Iranian Government has consistently been that the Baha'is are a political sect, allied to the interests of Zionism and United States Imperialism. These charges have presumably been adduced in order to avoid the implications of persecution on the grounds of religion. The Islamic Government of Iran therefore refuses to acknowledge the Baha'i Faith as a legitimate religion. On 12 September 1979, The Consulate General of the Islamic Republic of Iran answered a letter from an inquirer wishing to know the facts concerning the destruction of the House of the Bab in Shiraz. This reply indicates the tenor of response from Iranian Government representatives to the issue of the Baha'is in their country.

In the Name of Allah

'The general opinion of the Islamic Republican Government of Iran over the Moslems' reactions against Bahaie and Bahaieism.

1) The Ali Mohammad Bob's residence which is also his birthplace, was demolished by groups of people on the 8th September, 1979 (17th Shahrivar, 1358). The above incident coincided with the first anniversary of the martyred Iranian revolutionaries on the Bloody Black Friday when Iranians throughout the country were completely overwhelmed both in mourning and demonstrating against Israel, whose mercenaries had directly participated in the massacre of the gallant defenceless people of Shiraz.

    In the circumstances, to control the people's feelings from demolishing Ali Mohammad Bob's residence was impossible, and any interference from either the security forces or the residence's protective guards would have resulted in a great number of innocent people loosing [sic] their lives in Shiraz.

2) The Islamic Republic of Iran whose state religion is Shieh cannot and must not recognize and approve what is considered to be the unjust, creative and ruthless sect, such as Bahaies, who have close attachment and affinity to the universal zionism and is not regarded in minority religions, namely Christianity, Judaism and Zoroastrianism all of which are recognized by the council of constitutional experts.

    Taking the short history of the Bahaies' sect into consideration, it will be seen that this disturbing formation was produced by the Tsarist Russia and the British Imperialists; supported and subsidized by Israel as well as the Imperialism of America. Bahaieism is based on vain imagination and contributes nothing but will only create disunion with the more intellectual and ever increasing power of Islam.

    Above all, the Bahaies' destructive activities and their

manifest spying to the benefit of the foreigner, signifies
the faithful association of this sect as a politically
traitorous party with the international zionist regarded
as the overwhelming enemy to Islam and the creator of
Palestine's destitution.

Since it has repeatedly announced that the Islamic
Revolution of Iran intends to fight against the universal
zionism, Bahaies cannot be recognized, regardless the
conspicuous doctrinal proofs, as a minority religion, and
be approved of in the same way as the other minority
sects. The assemblees [sic] of the Bahaies' sect has [sic]
always been the spy centre and our Islamic nation will
never stand for such contaminated nests.

(from the Consulate of the Islamic Republic
of Iran, Manchester)

This document can be supplemented by the following
extract from a letter to a private American citizen, dated
October 15, 1979, and headed: Embassy of the Islamic
Republic of Iran, Washington D.C.

This may be difficult to face and realize that this issue
[i.e. the sacking of the House of the Bab] is not one of
religion, or of any minority, but a matter of certain
persons, be they Moslem, Christian, Jew, or Bah'ai, who,
in fact, cooperated with the deposed Shah's regime.
According to available documents which will be published, the ex-Shah had ordered to replace [sic] the
employees of the Government agencies such as all the
Iranian Airlines ... with Baha'is, and even to replace
the Armenians.

This letter then goes on to name prominent figures in the
Shah's regime who were active in SAVAK and at court, com-
mitting 'anti-people', 'anti-Islamic' actions, and stresses the
point that they were all Baha'is.

This idea of corruption fostered by Baha'is within the
Shah's regime, and dwelling on a few individuals, some of
whom were not Baha'is at all, is therefore the foundation of

the revolutionary authorities' case against the Baha'is. That it
is inaccurate in its discrimination of who were and who were
not Baha'is is the first point to be made against it. But its
major failing is its complete ignoring of the rest of the
300,000 or more Baha'i Community — individuals are always
easy to attach blame to — and the overwhelming majority of
political and non-political appointees in the Shah's regime, it
should be remembered, consisted of Muslims. The charge that
the Shah was about to replace the employees of Government
agencies, including all the Iranian airlines, with Baha'is, is a
puerile one, and could never be substantiated. The Baha'is
have expressed their point of view in the booklet, *Baha'is in
Iran*:

'Immediately following the Islamic Revolution, a campaign
began to hunt down the Baha'is and have them discharged
from both public and private employment. Civil servants who
had served their country faithfully for many years were
summarily dismissed from their jobs and denied back pay and
pensions solely on the grounds of their membership in what
was described as "the depraved Baha'i religion". In all such
cases Baha'is were told that if they denied their faith, their
rights would be restored. Among the first to be dismissed
were large numbers of Baha'i schoolteachers, who were
accused of corrupting the morals of their pupils. Pressure was
put on non-Baha'i employers to dismiss their Baha'i employees, and the majority concurred.

'Incited by the mullahs, riotous mobs in a number of cities
and towns looted Baha'i businesses of all kinds and, in many
cases, wantonly destroyed them. Others were confiscated by
the government, which also froze the business and personal
bank accounts of Baha'is. In the rural areas, the livestock and
crops of Baha'i farmers were stolen or destroyed. Armed
mobs invaded, looted and either occupied or destroyed
Baha'i homes throughout the country. Thousands were made
homeless as a result.

'Unable to support themselves or their families, thousands
of Baha'is have been forced to quit Iran, leaving behind all
their assets, to settle in other countries. Very large numbers
have been deprived of their means of livelihood and are now

existing under condtions of increasing hardship and degra-
dation.

'The campaign of physical intimidation has resulted in
countless Baha'is being terrorized both in the streets and in
their homes. Baha'i children have been vilified and beaten by
their fellow students and expelled from their schools. Elderly
men and women have suffered beatings, torture, and sometimes death at the hands of mobs.

'Among the most notorious of the many incidents of
violence to date have been the assassination of the internationally respected Baha'i physician, Professor Hakim of
Tehran University, who was gunned down in his office, and
the murders in the village of Nuk of Khurasan of Muhammad
Husayn and Shikkar-Nisa Ma'sumi, who were drenched with
kerosene and burned to death by a gang of fifteen masked
men.

'In every case where a Baha'i has faced execution by order
of a revolutionary court, and in many other instances where a
Baha'i has faced violence or death at the hands of mobs, he
(or she) has been offered the opportunity of saving himself
by recanting his faith. Wide publicity has been given to the
recantation in court of one of the members of the community and of a handful of Baha'is who recanted their faith
under duress. In the vast majority of cases, however, the
Iranian Baha'is have preferred to die rather than renounce
their beliefs.'

The report then goes on to deal with the allegation made
against Baha'is, which it describes as false, and springing
'from misunderstanding and deliberate misinterpretation of
the aims and purposes of the Baha'i Faith':

'The allegation that the Baha'is supported and benefited
from the former regime is founded upon the fact that the
Baha'i community did not denounce the Pahlavi regime or
affiliate itself with political organizations opposed to the
regime, and that a small number of Baha'is were appointed to
prominent positions in the civil service of that regime.

'In accordance with the teachings of their Faith, Baha'is
must show loyalty and obedience to the government of the
country in which they live, whatever its form or policies.

Accordingly, they do not engage in subversive activites. In addition, Baha'is are forbidden by the laws of their Faith from becoming involved in partisan politics or from holding any political post. These principles are fundamental and do not change with changing governments.

'The conduct of the Baha'ai community during the previous regime was therefore — as it continues to be today in the Islamic Republic of Iran — characterized by loyalty and obedience to the government, and by abstention from any partizan activities. So fundamental is the principle of not accepting any political post that, in one case under the Pahlavi regime, when a Baba'i accepted appointment as a Cabinet Minister, he was expelled from the Baha'i community.*

'Although a number of individual Baha'is because of their ability and integrity, were assigned by the former government to important posts in such fields as medicine, management, and administration, the Baha'i community as a whole suffered sustained and systematic discrimination throughout the Pahlavi regime.'

Baha'is in Iran refers to the points already made in *Chapter Two*, showing that Baha'i association with Israel is a result of historical accident, not Zionist links, and pointing out that the former SAVAK official Parviz Sabeti was not a Baha'i, and that no evidence exists to show any link between SAVAK and the Baha'is. It adds that Baha'is are not anti-Islamic as their opponents have claimed, but on the contrary, 'the Baha'i Faith is the only independent world religion, apart from Islam itself, which recognizes Muhammad as a Prophet of God, and the Holy Koran as a divinely revealed book. For a Baha'i to oppose, belittle or seek to destroy Islam, would thus be a denial of one of the most fundamental Baha'i principles.' As for the charges of immorality: 'these . . . have their roots in the differing social teachings of the Muslim and Baha'i religions. They spring from misunderstanding of the basic Baha'i principle of the equality of men and women, and rest solely upon the fact that . . . there is no

* see page 45, footnote.

segregation of men and women during Baha'i gatherings, and that women, as well as men, serve on Baha'i administrative bodies ... Furthermore, since the Baha'i marriage ceremony is not recognized in Iran and no civil marriage exists, Baha'is have been faced with two alternatives: either to deny their Faith and be married according to the rites of one of the recognized religions of the country, or to be honest and married according to Baha'i rites only. They chose the latter course. The present regime has regarded this course of action as prostitution.'

The truth of the respective positions in this debate is not hard to apportion, given the shifting sands upon which the authorities' case is built, and the dearth of evidence they have presented thus far to support their case. On the one hand, the authorities refuse to acknowledge Baha'is as followers of a bona fide, independently constituted religion, called them instead a political sect, but on the other, they have spoken of Baha'ism as a depraved 'religion', and exerted every pressure on Baha'is to re-convert to Islam. The reference to Baha'i collaboration under the Shah is a grotesque exaggeration of fact — Baha'i claims that none of their number occupied political posts are verifiable. The most that can be said for the authorities' argument is that individual Baha'is (not even a handful, and minute compared to the involvement of Muslims) were overtly powerful in economic terms during the Shah's regime. This has had unwarranted adverse effects on the vast majority of Baha'is who are entirely innocent, if this indeed is the cause of the charges thrown at the Baha'is. But in reality the motivation can be sought in a more basic factor: in the remarks of the Ayatollah Khomeini whilst in the West, there is to be found an association of the Baha'is (alongside the Christian missions) with the baneful influence of Western values upon Iranians, particularly the young. The fact is that Baha'is present a constant reminder to the more fanatical Shi'ite elements of the forces of the modern world against which they are fighting.

In fact the Baha'is, with their relatively good moral standing and abstinence from alcohol, often stood out from the Iranian society around them, in which the observance

of Islam was all the time declining under the Shah. In its
jealousy, the political arm of Shi'ism, created and supported
by the clerics, has turned upon the Baha'is with particular
vindictiveness, and has broken many of the principles of
Islam which it in theory professes. Above all, in their attempt
to get Baha'is to recant their faith, these Shi'ihs have contra-
vened the teaching of the Qur'an that there is no compulsion
in religion, and have utterly reneged on the once high standards cf tolerance associated with Islam in its early period.
In fighting against the Baha'is moreover, the cowardliness of
the persecutor reaches its nadir — for the Baha'is, unlike
other embattled elements in Iran today, will not defend
themselves, but are obliged by their faith to suffer without
retaliation. The regime of Ayatollah Khomeini, therefore,
must be viewed on its record not only of executing children
and old people, but in its attempt to uproot a pacific, law-
abiding community that has no recourse to justice, and no
opportunity to defend itself.

The Persecution of Babis and Baha'is in Iran:
A Chronology

1844	opposition of the Islamic clergy begins
1846	imprisonment of the Bab
1847	encirclement and killing of more than 300 Babis
1850	the Bab is martyred
1852	Baha'u'llah is imprisoned
	organized massacre in Tehran under the command of the Shah
1853	Baha'u'llah is exiled
1880	public killing of 2 distinguished Baha'is in Isfahan
1896	Nasirid-Din Shah assassinated by pan-Islamic terrorist, several Baha'is falsely accused and put to death
1902/3	100 massacred in Yazd
1906	outbreak of revolution precipated new attacks on Baha'is all over Iran
1930/50	Baha'i schools closed
	Baha'i marriages refused recognition
	Baha'i literature banned
	gatherings prohibited
	several Baha'is murdered
	Baha'i teachers, nurses, doctors, and government employees dismissed
1955	large scale attack on Baha'i community, fanatical Ayatollah whips mobs into frenzy
	Baha'i national headquarters taken over and demolished
	Minister of the Interior proclaims the Baha'i Faith banned
	House of the Bab desecrated and severely damaged
	bodies of Baha'is in cemeteries disinterred and mutilated
	shops and farms plundered, crops burned and livestock destroyed
	young Baha'i women abducted and forced to marry Muslims

children mocked, reviled, beaten and expelled from schools

hapless villagers boycotted by butchers and bakers

pressure brought upon Baha'is to recant their Faith

1979 Baha'i Faith not recognized by new regime, unleashing fresh persecutions

300 homes looted, burned and destroyed

clinic belonging to Baha'i doctors dynamited

Baha'i centres demolished and razed to the ground

individuals and families beaten

Baha'is dragged to mosques in efforts to force them to recant their Faith

the House of the Bab, holiest Baha'i shrine in Iran demolished

hundreds of Baha'is dismissed from government departments and denied the right to work

retired government employees denied pensions

1980 Ayatullah Saduqi calls on Baha'is in government departments to be identified, removed and handed over to revolutionary courts

Baha'i teachers under the Ministry of Education are dismissed

Baha'i marriages declared null and labelled prostitution

newly born babies from Baha'i familes not issued birth certificates

confiscation of Baha'i holy places

confiscation of companies owned by Baha'is

Baha'i hospital taken and interned elderly Baha'i patients thrown out

27 prominent Baha'is in Tehran, Tabriz, Kirman, Shiraz and Yazd arrested

elderly Baha'i in Birjand savagely killed because he refused to recant his Faith

four Baha'is tried by a revolutionary court and executed, based upon mere "confession" to being Baha'i

Chairman of the local Baha'i group in Tabriz and a well known local doctor charged with being Baha'is and executed

nine members of the National Assembly of Iran plus two other Baha'is arrested and abducted to an unknown destination

seven Baha'is in Yazd, central Iran, executed

1981   assassination of Professor Hakim in his Tehran clinic

execution of prominent Baha'is in batches in Shiraz, Hamadan and Tehran, bringing number of executions to 96, at the same time as arrests rose to over two hundred

continuation of policy of dismissing Baha'is from employment, removing licences to trade, etc.

denial of education to Baha'i students forced to declare their religion on forms of application

methods inaugurated whereby Baha'i community would be isolated under forthcoming registration laws

instruction to overseas embassies and consulates of Iran not to renew the passports of Baha'is

arrest of six members of Baha'i Assembly in Tehran

12 Documents relating to the official campaign of discrimination against the Baha'is. (reproduced from Baha'i publication: *"The Baha'is in Iran"*).

cular Letter from the Office of the Ministry Education

ferring to Decree No. 14973/2 dated 1st Tir '58 and in view of your not being a follower one of the official and recognized religions of ' country, you were thus dismissed from the nistry of Education; we state the following

e Ministry of Education, which has come into ng only through the justice of the Islamic public of Iran and the blood and martyrdom thousands of Muslims, men and women, not tolerate, like the previous regime, the stence of followers of the Bahá'í sect in its ucational unit, and in this way defile and viate the minds and thoughts of innocent dents.

view of the fact that, to the extent to which environment of education is pure and defiled, the schools can be mirrors of the lgent splendours of God, no doubt it cannot tolerated that, as under the previous regime, Bahá'ís should be active in the educational vities of the country. If you remember how y thousands of men and women according he guidance of the Muslim Ulamas suffered xile, and eventually quaffed the chalice of tyrdom, you will justly conclude that the y threshold of education should not be left eople like yourself, who are against the best rests of Islam and are spreading false ideas.

onclusion, I would like to remind you that employment of Iranians who are not follow- of recognized religions, such as Muslims, s, Christians and Zoroastrians, in Govern- t Offices is against the law.

refore, your dismissal according to the ting law is a minimum punishment. No bt the maximum punishment will befall e who employed you — who very shortly be tried in the Islamic Revolutionary Court. r previous salary payments made to you nst the law are being considered, and in re the result of this will be announced to

ned)

ammad 'Alí Rajá'í,* Guardian of the Minis of Education of the Islamic Republic of Iran

er Prime Minister of Iran

Article from the 18 February 1980 issue of the newspaper *Etela'at*

In this article, the director of the Department of Education in Eastern Adhirbáyján, Dr. Nayyri-vand, is quoted as saying:

"During this week, 30 persons employed in the Department of Education in this province who have collaborated with SAVAK, and 50 who are Bahá'ís, have been dismissed from their jobs . . . If the Bahá'ís accept Islam, they will again be employed and can return to their former jobs; otherwise, their files will be sent to the Revolutionary Courts in Tabriz for investigation."

12b

Article from the 30 June 1980 issue of the
newspaper *Jumhuri-i-Islami*

از سوی آیت‌الله ربانی شیرازی، آیت‌الله
دستغیب و آیت‌الله محلاتی:

پرداخت پول بیت‌المال به بهائیان حرام اعلام شد

شش نفر دیگر هم حکم آماده
بـخدمت صادر شده‌است وی
همچنین افزود چهل و چهارنفر
هم بجرم اعتقاد بمسلک بهائیت
بـاتوجه بـماده ۴۴۰ قـانون
استخدام کشوری اخراج شدهاند

همچنین طبق اطلاعات واصله
عدهای از کارمندان اداره آموزش
و پرورش فارس که بجرم بهائیت
اخراج شده بودند وزارت آموزش
و پرورش به این کار اعتراض کرد
و اعلام داشت کـه پـس از
بازنشستگی صدور احکام دیگر
وجه قانونی ندارد درتماسی که
با آیت‌الله دستغیب و آیت‌الله
ربانی و آیت‌الله محلاتی گرفته
شد درمورد پرداخت پول به
بهائیان اعلام کردند پرداخت
پول بیت‌المال به اینگونه اشخاص
حرام و کسانیکه از این فرمان
تمرد کند خاطی می‌باشد.

شیـراز ـ خـبرنگار.
جمهوری‌اسلامی: بـدنبال
پاکسازی در اداره‌جات دیروز از
طرف اداره آموزش و پرورش
استان فارس اعلام شد که تاکنون
به نود و شش پرونده رسـیدگی
شده و رای در مورد آنها صادر
شده‌است و جهت رسیدگی به
رای نهائی از طرف کمیسیون
پنج‌نفری مرکز به وزارت آموزش
و پـرورش ارسال شده‌است و

همچنین آقای ابوالاحراری مدیر
کل آموزش‌وپرورش استان اضافه
کرد تاکنون درحدود بیست
پرونده رای نهائی صادر شده
است که چهارده نفر آنها اخراج،
سه نفر به اتهام همکاری بـا
ساواک پرونده آنها بـدادگاه
انقلاب‌اسلامی شیراز ارجاع شده
است و شش نفر هم بـاز نشسته
شدهاند و درمـورد چهل و

12d

The article states that, following the "purifica-
tion project" of the government offices, and
"according to article 440 of the Government
Employment Act", 44 employees of the Ministry
of Education in the province of Fars were
dismissed "because of their belief in Bahaism".

The article goes on to state that, apparently
because of the protests of those dismissed, three
Ayatollahs (Mahalátí, Rabbáni and Dast-i-ghayb)
were asked to issue an edict about the payment
of pensions to Bahá'í ex-employees. The article
reads: "They (the Ayatollahs) have announced
that payment of any money from the treasury
to this kind of people is forbidden, and those
who do not observe this edict will be considered
as offenders."

12c   12e

13 Professor Manuchihr Hakim, assassinated by Islamic
revolutionaries, 12 January 1981.

14 Dr. Samandari of Tabriz who died in front of the
firing squad on 14 July 1980.

15   Yusuf Subhani, executed in Tehran, 27 July 1980.

16 Habibu'llah Azizi with his two sons.

17   Funeral of Habibu'llah Azizi—executed in Tehran, 29 August 1981.

18   Dr. Masih Farhangi.

19 Coffin of Dr. Masih Farhanghi, executed Tehran, 24 June 1981.

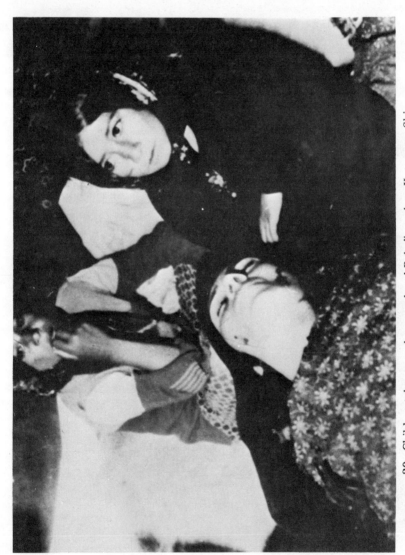

20 Child watches over her murdered Baha'i mother, Kata, near Shiraz.

21   Baha'i refuge camp — Kata, near Shiraz.

22   Seven Baha'is of Hamadan who were executed after torture of six,
     14 June 1981.

23   Shrine of the Bab on Mt. Carmel in Israel.

CHAPTER FIVE

Destroying the Defenceless

The Persecution of the Baha'is:
2. October 1980 to October 1981

According to an article by Eric Rouleau, in *Le Monde*, 24 June 1980, Ayatollah Sadoughi during a Friday sermon in Yazd referred to the Baha'is in the following terms:

> ... the venerable ayatollah called on the masses of the faithful to "evict the Baha'is whom you know from all administrative posts and turn them over to the revolutionary prosecutor".

The Ayatollah had already repeated the usual charges against Baha'is that they "were plotting in every city in Iran", says Rouleau: 'no doubt on behalf of the United States, Israel and the Shah ...' Sadoughi's words were g' en further coverage when published in *Etela'at* on 22 June.

Cables from Baha'is the world over to Khomeini, Bani-Sadr, and the Revolutionary Council, met with no response. By the new year (1981) dismissal of Baha'is from their employment had instead intensified. Although it is true to say that the clerics are at the forefront of the persecutions, political forces across the breadth of Iranian society have said nothing in support of Baha'is — except when it suited their political purposes. Indeed, so deep-seated is the prejudice against the Baha'is in Iranian society, that it can be said with relative certainty, that any new power in Iran is likely to denounce its previous, defeated opponents as Baha'is, The credence given to the charge of spying levelled against Baha'is is so widespread that attempts to enlighten at least the more conscientious sectors of Iranian society to the injustice of the treatment of Baha'is appear likely to fall on deaf ears.

Vicious as had been the oppression against this religious minority, knowledge concerning its religious character and general beliefs is as scarce as ever in today's Iran, even among the educated. For well over one hundred years the sources of information available have been poisoned by stories of foreign involvement in the spread of the Baha'i Faith; in a country for so long manipulated by outside powers, nationalism has demanded some scapegoat: like the Jews in Europe after 1918, the Baha'is represent just such a convenient scapegoat. Those who were more political in their analysis could always gloss their prejudice with references to the 'parasitical' behaviour of Baha'i businessmen. A hidden conspiracy to degrade Iran could always be attributed to the Baha'is. Anti-Baha'i feeling is as prevalent in Iran today as anti-Semitism was in Germany and the lands that comprised the old Austro-Hungarian Empire after World War One.

Given this background, how serious are the growing threats to Iran's Baha'is to be taken? Could the Baha'is in fact suffer the same fate as Europe's Jews? Those who doubt that the persecution of the Baha'is is being orchestrated in an organized way might question the realization of these worst fears — no evidence exists that definitely points to a plot of mass extermination, and could such a plot be carried out? That the persecution of the Baha'is has progressed in stages this book has so far given evidence to support — first occupation of Baha'i premises and seizure of assets, next dismissal of Baha'is from employment and denial of pension rights, then execution of prominent 'leadership'. What would the next stage be, beside the continuation of the others? We shall see that harassment and executions continued from October 1980 to the corresponding month of 1981; a fourth stage might also be discerned in the official measures steadily being taken to isolate the Baha'is from the rest of Iranian society by discriminatory laws, not only reducing them to the bad years' predicaments they suffered under Pahlavi monarchs, but suggesting preparation for rendering them, in terms of the law, effectively 'non-existent'. Without any recognition by the law, without passports to leave the country, discriminated against as 'heretics unacceptable to Islam', thousands of Baha'is might even now be waiting to tread the way to extinction.

The motivation for such a holocaust is not far to seek in the aims of the Shi'ite clergy: their goal has always been the creation of a theocratic, Islamic state — 'Islamic' to the extent that they have understood Islam. No religious minority would really be accepted kindly in such a state — Christians and Zoroastrians might be accepted under sufferance, but Baha'is, present in the midst of the theocratic community, would constitute an impossible grouping. Their very presence would stand against the basic premise of the Shi'ite clergy — that Muhammed is the last messenger from God, that the Imamate which was his legitimate successor is now under the custodianship of the ayatollahs themselves. The Baha'is, with their belief in the superseding of the whole Islamic dispensation by that of Baha'u'llah, the Mihdi and return of Imam Husayn, are simply intolerable to the ayatollahs' theocratic state, and can only be eliminated.

The complete failure of outside opinion to have any effect on the repressive activities of the Islamic Republican regime is in itself further testimony to the fanatical and impervious single-mindedness of the Shi'ite clerics now ruling Iran. Although Baha'is worldwide have lobbied political leaders and resolutions have been passed in the Spring and Summer by the Australian, Canadian, West German, and European Parliaments, the fear remains that such efforts are seen as further evidence of the close association of the Baha'is with Western Powers. Or if the Islamic regime in Iran is sensitive to adverse world opinion on account of persecution of minorities within its state, this has barely manifested itself in any staying of the hand of oppression.

In the first six months of 1981 more Baha'is suffered execution before firing squads than the whole previous year. The fateful date was 17 March, when two Baha'is suffered execution in Shiraz. The usual charges of collaboration with the Shah, espionage activities on behalf of Israel, and complicity in plots against the state were supplemented by outright reference to the fact that both accused were active Baha'is. The Revolutionary Court of Shiraz's verdict was subsequently confirmed by the Supreme Court in Tehran. The verdict was widely reported in an article published in the newspaper, *Jumhuri-i-Islami*, 18 March 1981, which included a press release from the Court of Shiraz: 'The Court of the Islamic Revolution of Shiraz examined the charges concerning two individuals named Mihdi Anvari son of Masih, and Hidayatu'llah Dihqani son of Nasru'llah from Abadih of Shiraz, and after a few days of trial, issued the necessary verdict which is the following:

'The first defendant *who was a member of the National Consultative Baha'i body* ... and together with his father belonged to the poets and sycophants of the defunct Shah and his father's court ... [accuses him of collaborating with SAVAK and being active against Muslims] and had contacts with Baitul Mal [presumably Baitul Adl, the Baha'i Universal House of Justice] in Haifa, the espionage centre of Zionism in Israel ... [accuses him of plotting with Colonel Vahdat]. The second defendant *who was a very active member of the Baha'i Assembly of Abadih* collaborated with Colonel Vahdat [and was responsible for converting Muslims to Baha'is] and in corrupting ignorant people especially peasants ...'

Membership in Baha'i institutions was for the first time made a capital offence by this verdict, and the precedent has been followed in all subsequent cases. In April, three more Baha'is were sentenced and executed in Shiraz. Then in June, the most bloody month yet, fourteen Baha'is died before firing squads; seven in Hamadan, after the torture of six of them, on 14th; and seven in Tehran, on 23rd and 24th. Among those who died in Tehran was Dr. Masih Farhangi, a noted member of the Baha'i guiding and protective body for Western Asia (called a 'Counsellor'). These losses were followed in July with the execution of another nine in Tabriz. Another Baha'i, Habib 'Azizi, of Bournemouth, U.K., was executed in Tehran on 29 August. Several members of his family, including his aged mother, were subsequently arrested. Mr. 'Azizi had spent more than a year in prison —

his place was taken by other Baha'is arrested in a constant flow since active persecution on the part of the authorities against individual Baha'is began in late 1979. By October the figure for the execution of Baha'is under the Islamic regime was estimated at ninety-six. Several hundred had been arrested.

This premeditated campaign proceeded at the same time as mass executions of political opponents of the regime (and suspects and innocent people no doubt) gained the attention of the world's media. The Baha'is were undoubtedly the most hard pressed minority, although prominent Jews and Christians had lost their lives, including the son of the Anglican Bishop of Tehran. In the apparent chaos of execution and counter-assassination, the Baha'is were just one group suffering anguish in a country filled with fear and mourning. Yet they knew that once the clerics effectively established their dictatorship, and had political opponents under their feet, they would then be in a position to turn all their force against the Baha'is. While the struggle for power went on, the Baha'is could be left to wait in apprehension, unable to leave the country legally, or to marshal means of defence.

In the meantime, despite the evidence of the report of the Court of Shiraz and subsequent arraignments against Baha'is, the authorities still maintained no one was being killed in Iran for their beliefs, but Baha'is who had been sentenced had died because of their political activities. Thus the following report from *Etela'at International*, dated 5 August 1981, and headed: 'No-one is executed in Iran for their beliefs':

> In response to the intelligence reported by the French News Agency, that two young Baha'i girls have been kidnapped in Iran, Reza Alavi, spokesman for the Iranian Islamic Republic's Ministry of Foreign Affairs, said in an interview with the Paris News Agency: 'In addition to denying this falsehood perpetrated by the French News Agency, we announce that such reports at this time are merely incriminating excuses used by the French Government to give asylum to Bani-Sadr, Rajavi and their accomplices'.
> The spokesman for the Ministry of Foreign Affairs also referred to the rumoured executions of Baha'is in Iran

and said: 'Such intelligences which are reported by the
Zionist news agencies with excessive zeal are without
foundation, and it must be said that in Iran no-one is
executed for their beliefs, and those who to this day
have been executed were connected with Zionist organisations and the spies of the CIA'.

More or less the same response *vis-à-vis* the charge of execution of Baha'is for their belief is to be found in the following letter from the Embassy of the Islamic Republic of Iran,
London, to Mr. Ken Weetch, Member of Parliament for
Ipswich. It is worth quoting in full if only as evidence that
the front of the authorities remained the same even during
the month of its worst persecution of Baha'is to date:

Dear Sir,
    With reference to your letter of 22nd June, 1981, I
would like to draw to your kind attention the following
points:
    Bahaism is in fact not a religion but an ideology
created by colonial powers to help the past illegitimate
government of Iran in their oppressions of the brave
people of Iran and to invalidate Islam as a divine religion
and revolutionary ideology.
    Before the revolution especially at the time of the
Shah, Baha'is have cooperated with this government to
oppress people and to plunder our country's wealth.
The majority of people who had occupied high positions
during the Shah's power, such as his Prime Minister
Hovida and many high rank military officers were
Bahais.
    Notwithstanding the above-mentioned facts, the
Government of the Islamic Republic of Iran has never
oppressed them, although their beliefs have not and will
never be considered as a recognized religion by Iranian
authorities and therefore, unlike Chrisitans, Jews etc.
they do not have priorities such as the right to elect
representatives for the Parliament.
    If some people who have been executed have hap-
pened to be Bahais, or, if some properties confiscated
by the Islamic Courts have happened to be Bahais'
belongings, this does not mean that the Islamic Government is oppressing them. Considering the fact that most
criminals who were executed by the orders of the

Islamic Courts have been so-called Muslims, I am sure this does not mean that the Iranian authorities are oppressing true Muslims or non-Muslims if they have not been criminals.

I hope this summary would help you to appreciate the justice being implemented by the Islamic Republic of Iran based on the Quranic principles against unjustice [sic].

signed Alireza Farrokhrouz
Chargé d'Affaires

The penultimate paragraph of the letter is particularly insidious when it is known that seven Baha'is in Hamadan had suffered torture and execution barely nine days before the letter had been written, and that seven more were to die almost at the exact time — in every case, opportunity for release existed for the victims would they only recant their religion.

With the executions, another pattern of persecution was being laid: it is this that may ultimately yield the ultimate fruit — the removal of the Baha'is from Iran in toto. The method of achieving this would be to use the recognized religions as the criterion for registration of the entire Iranian population; and since the Baha'is would be unable to identify themselves as belonging to one of these, their previous lack of recognition under the constitution of the Islamic Republic would then become an acknowledge fact. Legal means would be used, in other words, to isolate the Baha'i minority completely, and the cover would be the constitution of the country which the new laws could be said to be merely reinforcing. The precarious position Baha'is have always been under implicitly in Iran would then be made explicit; their disqualification under the law would not just mean the non-recognition of their marriages, it would make their holding jobs, property, bank accounts, and businesses, illegal. The benefits of this procedure for the government lie in the fact that it can be pursued under the same terms of reference as all other pogroms of Baha'is in Iran in the past. Baha'is have not had recognition in their own country in the hundred and thirty years of their existence; they have been disabled under every constitution Iran has had in that period. The Islamic Republic of Iran can take advantage of a history of repression and a widespread hatred among the population to rid Iran finally of those it represents as the sworn enemies of the Shi' ite religion.

The process has already begun. Baha'is have been summoned to appear before a court in Yazd — in early August the Government froze the assets of 117 Baha'is in Yazd, and subsequently ordered the heads of 150 prominent Baha'i families to report to the revolutionary authorities. If any of these failed to turn up before the given date, repercussions were threatened. The Baha'is appeared as bidden only to find the order had been changed. The serious implications behind this chain of events are not diminished by the apparently neutral outcome — why make the order at all? Moreover, some of the names called were of people already dead — showing that the names had been obtained from lists taken from the Baha'is themselves, and did not represent persons who had committed any crime.

Meanwhile the arrests continue — in October, a report spoke of Baha'is being imprisoned in Urumiyyih and Azerbaijan. In Masjid Sulaymen the authorities instructed banks to submit lists of all Baha'i accounts. Mob harassment and plundering goes on costing lives and property. Plans for the construction of a road and square on the site of the House of the Bab have been put forward despite the assurance of the revolutionary guards who took it over in 1979 that it was being held 'in trust'. In Birjand in Khurasan homes of Baha'is have been ransacked and the owners forced to flee into the desert. Baha'i workers have been increasingly expelled from factories, and licenses for Baha'i shopkeepers have been frequently withdrawn.

The children of Baha'is have not been exempt from suffering either. Teachers and inspectors have told other children to shun them, and have remonstrated with Baha'i children as young as ten and eleven over ideology. Teachers insult the outcasts, and even, as reported in one case, gave a child derogatory statements about its parents' faith to copy out. Above all, in the field of education, Baha'is are now suffering systematic discrimination. Registration forms of students applying for school and university places are closely scrutinized, and refusal of Baha'i students has resulted. Decree number 11397 dated September 30 1981 lists crimes which disqualify professors and students from being employed or registered at the universities: among the crimes listed is 'membership in sect which is recognized by Muslims as the misled heretical sect'.

Against this sombre background, the world's opinion has progressively aligned itself against the policies of the Iranian Government towards this hated minority. The great amount of diplomatic activity conducted by the Baha'is of the world is summarised in the report,

Baha'is in Iran

'First, the Baha'i International Community appealed to the United Nations Sub-Commission on Prevention of Discrimination and Protection of Minorities which, in a resolution of 10th September 1980, expressed its profound concern for the safety of the members of the Baha'i community in Iran and invited the government of Iran to protect the fundamental human rights and freedoms of this religious minority.

'On 19 September 1980, following appeals to its members by the Baha'i communities of Europe, the European Parliament unanimously adopted a resolution condemning the persecution of the Baha'is in Iran and calling upon the government to grant recognition to the Baha'i community.

'Also as a result of appeals by European Baha'is the Parliamentary Assembly of the Council of Europe published a Written Declaration on the plight of the Baha'is in Iran, calling upon the Committee of Ministers of the twenty-one Member States of the Council of Europe to make urgent representations to the Iranian authorities to put an end to the persecutions.

'Following the European Parliament resolution, the Foreign Ministers of several member governments of the European Communities informed the Baha'is of their own countries that the nine Member States of the European Communities shared the concern of the European Parliamentarians for the plight of the Iranian Baha'is. Since, however, efforts to improve the treatment of the Baha'is in Iran had met with no positive results, the Foreign Ministers of the Nine recommended that the Baha'i International Community take the matter to the human rights organs of the United Nations, where the support of the nine governments was assured.

'Acting on this recommendation, the Baha'i International Community made two statements to the 37th Session of the United Nations Commission on Human Rights, which met in Geneva from 2nd February to 13th March 1981.

'In its first statement, the Baha'i International Community drew the attention of the Commission to the kidnapping of three prominent Baha'is and to the arrest, and subsequent disappearance, of the nine members of the National Spiritual Assembly of the Baha'is of Iran and two appointed officers of the Baha'i Faith. In its second statement, the Baha'i International Community had the opportunity of describing the persecution in Iran and of emphasising the deliberate omission of the Baha'is from the Constitution and the systematic nature of the persecution.

'Many delegates from among the one hundred or so governments represented at the Commission were extremely sympathetic to the Baha'i case, and four governments – the Netherlands, Canada, Australia and the United Kingdom – made specific reference to the persecution of the Baha'is in Iran in general statements on the violation of human rights.

'Concerned that there had been no response from the government of Iran either to the appeals of Baha'is or of international bodies and governments, and increasingly anxious to stem the tide of persecution against their co-religionists, the Baha'is of Europe again appealed to the European Parliaments which, on 10 April 1981, adopted a second unanimous resolution on the Baha'i case, calling on the Foreign Ministers of the ten Member States of the European Communities to make the necessary representations to the Iranian government.' The report then mentions that the matter is to continue to receive the attention of the ten Member States. It continues:

'At the Spring 1981 session of the Economic and Social Council of the United Nations (ECOSOC), held in New York in April/May, the ten Member States of the European Communities drew attention to the plight of the Baha'is in Iran in a statement dealing with religious intolerance. The delegation of Canada also referred to the Baha'is in their comments on the same subject.' The section concludes:

'The appeals made and the information supplied by Baha'is throughout the world to the governments, parliamentarians, prominent officials and media in their own countries concerning the rapidly-worsening plight of their co-religionists in Iran have resulted in an ever-growing international awareness of the situation.

'The Parliaments of Canada, Australia and the Federal Republic of Germany have passed resolutions deploring the persecution of the Baha'is in Iran, and the matter has been debated in other national parliaments. Political leaders of many parties and religious leaders of many denominations have publicly denounced the persecutions and have expressed to the Baha'is in their country their sympathy and full support for their fellow-believers in Iran.'

A meeting was held at Westminster on 8 July in one of the committee rooms of the House of Commons. Members of Parliament from all parties attended and Stanley Clinton-Davis took the chair. Denis Healey and Julian Amery were followed by Senator Alan Missen from the Australian Senate, Lord McNair, and the Rev. Harding, Director of the U.K. United Nations Association. All of these speakers, as well as the other M.P.s who spoke, voiced their sense of outrage at what was happening to the Baha'i minority in Iran. Lord McNair in particular said the Baha'i Faith should commend itself to everyone, especially in its ethical beliefs: education, especially of women, employees sharing in the profits and responsibilities of the firms they work for, and the aspirations for world order he found particularly important. The Rev. David Harding promised the UNA would press for investigation by a Human Rights Commission and suggested a Parliamentary delegation be sent to Iran. Ideas differed however as to exactly how much could be done for the Baha'is in view of the bad standing Western countries — especially Britain — had in Iran. The point had been stressed earlier in a Commons reply by the Minister of State for Foreign and Commonwealth Affairs, Douglas Hurd. Asked (24 June) if he proposed to take any action on behalf of the British Government concerning the persecution of Baha'is in Iran, he replied: 'In all these matters, we must judge whether we can do anything that will help those concerned. It must be remembered that there is a widespread — but entirely wrong — impression in Iran that in the past the Bahais have been used for British political purposes. We must take that impression into account when deciding what could usefully be done.' And further — as in the past — though no one could doubt the concern of the British Government at the events in Iran going forward at the expense of the Baha'is, it still has its own political interests to consider, and might not wish to prejudice what influence it does have with Iran, an oil-producing state.

In 1955 and again in 1956, the United Nations had passed a resolution in support of the Baha'is — one which the then Iranian Government had eventually responded to. In September, a sub-commission of the United Nations Human Rights Commission sitting at Geneva passed a resolution condemning the 'systematic persecution' of the Baha'is. This subcommission is responsible for the rights of minorities, and it described the acts of persecution as 'motivated by religious intolerance and a desire to eliminate the Baha'i faith in the land it its birth.' The resolution found nineteen supporters, no opposers, and five abstainers. The Baha'is next goal must be to get a full-bloodied United Nations Resolution against Iran. In the meantime, in June, thirteen Masters and Wardens of Oxford University colleges signed an appeal to Kurt Waldheim urging international public opinion to do all it could to persuade the Iranian Government from pursuing its policies of persecution 'of these law-abiding, religious people, who are in no way involved in political matters.'

However, at the time of writing, all this diplomatic activity and publicity of the Baha'i case seems to have effected no let up in the process towards the goal of destruction of this minority. Two media reports in September and October, without giving their sources, suggested the Islamic regime was going ahead with plans that would isolate and enable the authorities to round up Baha'is. First Rosemary Righter, in the *Sunday Times*, 20 September 1981, in a story headed, 'Iran plans a final solution for 300,000 "rebels": death if they don't recant faith':

> Over the next few months Ayatollah Khomeini's regime will enforce new decrees that will make every aspect of their [the Baha'is] existence illegal. Baha'is who refuse to renounce their faith will be progressively isolated — and then, they fear, killed . . .
>
> The new laws will be based on Iran's Islamic constitution which recognises three smaller minority religions — Christianity, Judaism and . . . Zoroastrianism — but not the Baha'i Faith. Membership of one of the official religions will now be comprehensively enforced. Baha'is will thus be barred from holding jobs, owning property, having bank accounts, running businesses, getting medical treatment or travelling.
>
> Baha'i weddings are already not recognised as lawful. New legislation will make all Baha'is marriages, even those of 50 years' duration, null and void. Married couples will be considered as "involved in prostitution", a crime punishable by death. Baha'i children will become illegitimate and their parents will be deprived of all rights over them.
>
> The climax will come on March 20, when all Iranians are to register for new identity cards. Baha'is will not be eligible. They will thus be clearly singled out for "naboudi" (elimination) . . .

The second item was broadcast on 'Voice of America', 20 October 1981. The text is as follows:

> A report from Tehran says Iran's Central Revolutionary Committee is planning a new campaign to round up members of the Baha'i Faith. The Baha'is reportedly will be arrested on grounds that their marriages are

illegal and their children illegitimate since Iran does not recognize the Baha'i Faith. The Committee says some 96 Baha'is have been executed so far and another 200 are under arrest. Some 10,000 Baha'i families are believed to have fled Iran since the campaign against them began. The Committee has another 20,000 Baha'i names on its arrest list compiled from captured Baha'i office lists and documents from the Shah's old secret police SAVAK. Many Baha'is have changed their names or gone into hiding to escape capture.

Only subsequent events can prove or disprove the accuracy of such prognostications. The feeling among the Baha'is in Iran, needless to say, is of great trepidation. They have reason to fear added penalties against them out of vindictiveness, if their case is reported widely in the West, and political pressure is exerted on their behalf. Yet the alternative is certainly even darker — for if their case is forgotten, there can be little doubt that the religious dictatorship in Iran will be happy to eliminate their victims quietly. The scope of torture and execution in general under the Shi'ite fundamentalist regime is thus far unknown. The Baha'is have everything to fear if the spotlight of the world's media is turned off them — but such is the grim state of the world today that their cause might easily be passed over for another's. Past experience of the persecution of minorities in the world's history reveals, unfortunately, that the prevailing interests of governments at the time tended to make them wish for the problem to be put aside — or to put it more bluntly, it would be more convenient for the rest of mankind if those being presecuted merely accepted their fate silently.

CHAPTER SIX

Looking fearfully to the Future'

Le Monde

'Iran's Baha'is . . . are scapegoats for all ills.'
Paul Balta, *Le Monde*
Of all the minorities, Baha'is are the most
vulnerable . . .'   M.M.J. Fisher, *Iran From Religious
Dispute to Revolution*

What will happen to Iran's Baha'is? We have said that their
history of persecution is a significant, if hitherto unex-
plored, pointer to the state of Iranian society. Further, we
have seen how the traditional persecutors of the Baha'is have
been the Shi'ite clerics, and how the Islamic Republican
regime has tried to justify its oppression of the Baha'is by
calling them agents in the Shah's regime. For the clerics as
well as for the Baha'is, the events we have delineated taking
place in Iran, and which have by no means reached their
consummation yet, represent a climactic in terms of their
development. The future of Iran's Baha'is holds great significance for persecutors as well as persecuted; we need to consider the following factors in estimating what that future
holds:

1) the significance for the Islamic Republic of its persecution of Baha'is
2) the significance of this persecution for the Baha'is
3) the significance of the persecution for the rest of the
world.

1) The Revolution that overthrew the Shah was of course a
political revolution, but it was also a religious revolution too.

The aim of the fundamentalist clergy centered on Ayatollah Khomeini was the establishment of a theocratic state, in which politics would be the politics of God. That was the level at which they set the mark of their activities, and although it would probably be right to see more basic political motives involved as well, these Shi'ite clerics have wielded power in the name of God, and gone about extirpating their enemies in his name too. So, once the course of the anti-Shah revolution was set on this fundamental Islamic course, and taken away from opposition secular Muslim politicians like Sanjabi and Bazargan, it became increasingly shaped by the religious attitudes of the clerics of Iran's dominant religion.

The Shi'ite clerics include or have included conservative fundamentalists like Khomeini and Motahhari, and moderates like Shariatmadari and Taleghani. Khomeini's party has triumphed, and the Islamic Republic of Iran eventually became the regime of the Islamic Republican Party. It is fair to say that this represents the most rigid and fundamentalist grouping of Shi'ite clergy — those who would alone accept a theocratic state and would not bargain with secular politicians. Further, this religious political party embodies the historical hatred of the Baha'is on the part of Shi'ite clerics in its most intense form. It is wrong to say that all Shi'ite leaders indiscriminately have automatically attacked the Baha'is; but Khomeini's movement undoubtedly contains those elements who have historically persecuted the Baha'is — this we can see both from their ideas (the popular appellation of 'Imam' given to Khomeini is of course absurd to moderates like Shariatmadari, but is proof of the messianic aspect of Khomeini's Shi'ism which in turn must anathematize the Baha'i interpretation of the return of the Imams) and from their actions. The Islamic Revolution that overthrew the Shah threw up exactly that element in Iranian society that most hates the Baha'is. In the religious zeal of the Islamic Republican regime there must therefore have been expression of this old hatred — the opportunity had arisen for a jihad against an historical enemy that could never before have been conducted with such freedom of manoeuvre.

To add to the significance of this historic opportunity, the religious polarity, as we have suggested, seemed never more marked. At last the Shi'ite clerics held unfettered power themselves, and this power was wielded in the name of God — and God's politics, according to these Shi'ihs must sanction, or rather enjoin, the elimination of the 'depraved heretical sect' — the Baha'is.

There can be no doubt that the Islamic regime is persecuting the Baha'is for religious reasons then; but it has wisely developed a more subtle terms of reference for carrying out its design. The prejudice against the Baha'is that is found ubiquitously among intellectuals is that the Baha'is, while claiming to be non-political, are really the agents of foreign powers. The stigma also attaches to the Jews, Zoroastrians, and Christians Armenians, but whereas at least a few members of these minorities were to be found within the anti-Shah camp, no Baha'is were. The political prejudice against the Baha'is is therefore a good cloak to cover religious hatred, and popular belief attributes Baha'i membership to the most hated individuals in the Shah's regime. Here then is an excellent approach that could almost have been tailored to the wishes of the Shi'ite fundamentalists: the Baha'is were foreign spies and supporters of the Shah's most corrupt institution, SAVAK — these political charges are perfectly suited to prosecution and elimination of the Baha'is.

The political allegations made against the Baha'is are therefore motivated, on the part of the more fanatical and fundamentalist Shi'ites, by opportunist tactics, and are in reality a cloak to hide an inveterate religious prejudice. It is doubtful that the Baha'is would have been subject to the kind of pressures they have been under Khomeini had a secular grouping triumphed in the revolution. They would have been unlikely to have received any favours from such a regime, but on the other hand the religious hatred of a professedly religious government would have been absent.

The significance of the persecution of the Baha'is for the Islamic Republican regime of Iran is therefore built into its assumption of complete power in Iran: having at last the opportunity to carry out their principles in government, the mullas have attacked the Baha'is with all the new power at their disposal. If they were to lose this opportunity of destroying their enemy, they would scarcely hope for another in the future. On these terms then, the future for the Baha'is under the Islamic Republican regime looks very bleak.

2) For the Baha'is, the persecutions they have been suffering under the Islamic regime also represent a climactic in their history. The victims of periodic campaigns against them since their earliest years, the Baha'is have grown used to opprobrium and disablement. With their historical enemies and oppressors in power, the Baha'is have realized since the installation of Ayatollah Khomeini's regime in February 1979 that grim times lie ahead.

However, though they have had little alternative to passive acceptance of what their enemies decided to perpetrate against them, their suffering has not been in vain. The Baha'is in Iran now have the opportunity to show by their patience the unfair treatment they have continuously experienced in their homeland. The interest of the outside world in their case has been on a greater scale than even 1955. At last the world generally is being able to appreciate the bigotry and fanaticism this minority has faced for so long.

The Baha'is outside Iran have seized the chance both to acquaint governments and peoples with the plight of their fellow believers in Iran, and to explain the nature of the beliefs these Iranian Baha'is have been suffering for. As for Iran itself, the hope must be that by the heroic example of men like Professor Hakim, Dr. Samandari and Dr. Farhanghi, as well as many others who are not well known, the Iranian people may come to understand the high standards of these Baha'is — their tenacity of belief, and loyalty to their country.

The persecution of the Baha'is in Iran represents for them the occasion to emerge from the obscurity and oppression of over a century. It is paradoxical that the present sufferings of the Baha'is in Iran have within them the seeds of the emancipation of this minority in Iran. For however many have to die, others have pledged to take their place. This has been illustrated by the arrest of the National Spiritual Assembly, and the election of a new one. The authorities have indeed a gargantuan task before them if they really believe they can break the resolve of the Iranian Baha'i community by the cruel and cowardly methods they have adopted so far.

Those prominent Baha'is who have been tried and executed for their religious beliefs — and offered a pardon if they would recant — have demonstrated their faith, and endorsed the high standards of their religion. For the Baha'is are obedient to the government of their country in all things - except in matters fundamental to religion. The Baha'is do not practice *taqiyya*, or dissimulation of their faith as Shi'ites are allowed to; their position is in essence the same as the early Christians who refused to compromise their religion on pain of death. Baha'is have gone as far as to obediently disband their activities if bidden by a government (as in Nazi Germany and Soviet Russia where they were required to do so in the early 'thirties and late 'twenties respectively) — but they will not recant their belief, which is precisely what the persecution of the Shi'ite clerics aims at. The significance of the present persecution for the Baha'is is therefore its fundamental testing of their belief — not since the most vicious persecutions of the last century, have the Baha'is faced this trial on such a scale.

At the same time, the Baha'i Faith as a complete entity, constituting its worldwide following as well as that in Iran, has been brought increasingly to the attention of the world. Hitherto little regarded and often branded as a sect of Islam, the Baha'i Faith is coming to be seen as a genuine religion, independent, and on a par with the older recognized religions of the world.

The Baha'i community in Iran is being purified — reports speak of perseverance and steadfastness even among Baha'i children. Renewal of opposition has cleaned the dross from the community as well — those who had excessive wealth have either fled the country, or having lost virtually everything, have fallen back upon the resources of their religion. The cooperative virtues found in the Baha'i teachings have returned to the Baha'i community, and Baha'is are demon-strating to their fellow Iranians the value of brotherhood and egalitarianism.

The future for the Baha'i minority is likely to possess an inexpressible piquancy — if the roll-call of deaths rises into thousands, perhaps tens of thousands, the human suffering involved will be too tragic to consider. Yet Baha'is have faced martyrdom before, and have accepted it in the belief that their cause would thereby prosper. It is perhaps for the rest of mankind — for governments and international agencies in particular — to see that the Baha'is are not called upon to make such a sacrifice.

3) At a time in history when the recognition on the part of world opinion of the fundamental need for human rights has been accompanied by some of the most gross violations seen in recent times, the case of the Baha'is might seem just one among many threatened violations. The Baha'is have not engaged in politics and are not being removed because they represent an outright political threat to the Iranian Govern-ment. That is one of the most insidious factors about their case. The Baha'is are not religious fanatics who might destroy the equilibrium of the state either. On the contrary, wherever Baha'is reside they are found to be loyal and also progressive and creative citizens. Although they believe in the unity of the human race, they go about their beliefs quietly, without flaunting their opposition in reactionary or racist states. The nature of their non-political stance has not been understood because Baha'is have not advertised their views on this matter. Yet the Baha'i Faith has managed to spread to most countries of the world, with the exception of extremely exclusive states. This has been possible because of the very fact of the non-political, obedient character of Baha'i communities. Within the Baha'i communities themselves, the principles of racial interaction (including inter-racial marriage) and agreement, education, the emancipation of women, abstinence from alcohol and harmful drugs, co-operative and profit-sharing schemes especially in Third World countries, have progressively been implemented to the

benefit of the wider community. Baha'is are not exclusive or introverted in the divided society of Africa and Asia where race, religion, caste and tribe, severally or all together have such divisive effects.

Looking at the United Nations Charter of Human Rights, and at the Baha'i teachings, perfect agreement is to be found on nearly all points. The Baha'is loyally support the United Nations and are never to be found among its critics.

Can the world allow the Baha'is to be eliminated in the country of their birth, when they represent worldwide one of the most open-minded forward-looking groups extant in the world today? Oppression of defenceless minorities is a sickening matter wherever it occurs in the world. The Baha'is have asked for no special consideration or treatment; on the contrary, all they require are their basic human rights of freedom of belief, and the right to live unmolested and unthreatened. All human life is equally sacrosanct, and the lives of Baha'is are not to be placed above others — yet can the world really allow human beings with such enlightened views to be eliminated merely on account of those very beliefs?

In this last respect, the persecution of the Baha'is in Iran is a peculiarly pointed test of humanitarian strength and the concern of enlightened world opinion on human rights contravention. Looking back over the past century with its infamous instances of pogrom leading to massacre and annihilation, recalling the terrible fates of such scapegoats and villified minorities as the Jews, Armenians and Slavs, we may be inclined to feel pessimistic about the future of the Baha'is. We even saw how twenty thousand deaths went unrecorded in the early history of the Babi-Baha'i movement. Yet it remains true that the surest road to extermination is the one of meek acceptance and fatalism. We have said that Iran's Baha'is can do little more than accept with fortitude — on the rest of mankind the responsibility falls of raising a clamour, such a clamour that the present authorities in Iran will desist from their infamous strategem. The solidarity of the human race — on which Baha'is themselves place so much emphasis — must teach us this, otherwise the torch of enlightenment will be extinguished, and when oppression stalks the earth, no group or sector of society, no single man, can feel free.

POSTSCRIPT

The new year 1982 brought a yet more ghoulish turn in the secret pogrom being conducted against Iran's Baha'is; a new spate of arrests and executions swept away their top leadership, and accounted for fifteen lives, including three women.

In the middle of December, eight members of the National Assembly of the Baha'is of Iran meeting in a private house were seized, and sequestered away. A week or so later, the bodies of five, including one woman, were accidentally discovered in a graveyard reserved for 'infidels'. There could be no doubt that the entire body of the highest Baha'i authority in Iran, with the exception of one member absent from the above meeting, had been killed. This Assembly had been elected in August 1980 to replace the previous body which had disappeared that same month.* The decimation of the new Assembly made the fate of the previous one appear virtually sealed: it could only mean that two National Assemblies of the Baha'is had been eliminated in two separate massacres. The silence of the Iranian authorities in their turn when questioned on the whereabouts of the first and the charges levelled against the second, testified to their complicity in a series of barbarous and disgusting acts.

But there was to be yet more blood on their hands. On 4 January, six members of the Baha'i Local Assembly of Tehran, and the hostess in whose home they had been meeting when arrested in November 1981, were discovered to have been secretly executed. No charges had been brought against them — they had been surreptitiously and covertly massacred in the same manner as their brothers and sisters on

* see pp. 14-16.

the National Assemblies. These despicable deeds created waves of revulsion when reported in the media outside Iran, coupled as they were with the approaching registration date for Iranians on March 20, after which food would only be available to those carrying identity cards. Needless to say, these are being denied to Baha'is. With their institutions under ruthless seige, and their identity as Iranian citizens in the process of disappearing, the Baha'is now face the prospect of starvation.

Today the Baha'i Community of Iran is compassed by a Stygian gloom; the flower of its leadership is dead, cynically cut down by cowardly fusillades of bullets. Those who have died were no zealots or political terrorists, but all too quiet and respectable. The National Assembly of the Baha'is of Iran included two doctors, two lawyers, and a woman physicist. Neither were they glib Girondins dying on a public stage — their executioners did away with them in the unearthly hours, and buried them in common land, as murderers do their victims. These silent martyrs are testimony to a flagrant diabolism masquerading in the weeds of sanctity. Iran's 'Islamic' regime vies with the Medieval Inquisition in its satanic overturn of spiritual values: history, in appraising this regime of viperous clerics, will recall the words of Charlotte Corday, and say: 'Religion — what crimes are committed in thy name!' We might well wonder if the Baha'is, like the hapless Cathars, are fated to be slaughtered in their tens of thousands in the bloody upheavals yet to flood the land of their birth.

Geoffrey Nash, London,
January 1981.

Description of the Baha'i Faith

Baha'i Source

The Baha'i Faith

The Baha'i Faith is an independent world religion, dedicated to the promotion of a world civilisation characterised by the true brotherhood of man under the Fatherhood of God. Its name, Baha'i comes from the Founder, Baha'u'llah, and simply means 'a follower of Baha'u'llah'.

Origin of the Baha'i Faith

The Baha'i Faith arose in Persia (now Iran) in the middle of the 19th century.

The three Central Figures of the Baha'i Faith were The Bab (Siyyid 'Ali Muhammad) 1819–1850; Baha'u'llah (Mirza Husayn 'Ali) 1817–1892 and 'Abdu'l-Baha ('Abbas Effendi) 1844–1921. (also see pp. 143–146)

International Status of the Baha'i Faith

The Baha'is within the brief space of 136 years have established a world community. As of March 1980 they live in more than 106,000 localities in 360 countries, territories and island groups. Baha'i literature has been translated into more than 660 languages. Members of 1,820 different ethnic groups now comprise this international community, representing a true cross-section of the human race. Such is its virility, its power to demonstrate its spiritual truth and the effectiveness of its divinely-inspired Administration.

Another evidence of the world-wide stature of the Baha'i Faith is the variety and extent of its institutions and properties. Houses of Worship open to all peoples and embodying unique architectural designs have been built in Wilmette

(U.S.A.); Kampala (Uganda); Sydney (Australia); Frankfurt (Germany); and Panama City; others are in the process of construction in India and Western Samoa and national Temple sites have been purchased in over 120 countries. National Headquarters have been bought in nearly 130 countries and national endowments established in almost the same number. Twenty-three Baha'i Publishing Houses are in existence, and schools, teaching institutes and other institutions are established in many countries. Over 3,000 district and local endowments and headquarters have been acquired.

As an independent World Religion with it own Founders, Scriptures, Holy Days, Calendar, Houses of Worship and legally recognised in many countries around the world to perform marriages, observe its Holy Days, possess properties, cemeteries and endowments, it has made amazing progress since its birth in the predominantly Muslim environment of Persia.

Its relationship to Islam is similar to that which existed between Christianity and Judaism, being born into the earlier environment but quite independent from it. In its achievements to date, the Baha'i Faith has demonstrated that though its early surroundings were essentially Persian, the universal Message of Baha'u'llah merits recognition as the youngest and most virile of the world's independent living religions.

United Nations and the Baha'i Faith

The Baha'i Faith has accredited representation at the United Nations Headquarters in New York city both nationally and internationally.

The Baha'i International Community has been listed as an international N.G.O (Non-Governmental Organisation) since 1948. N.G.O.s provide grass-roots support of the United Nations, supplementary to that of governments in seeking to promote the goals of its Charter; peace, economic and social advancement of all peoples, and the promotion of human rights.

In 1970, the Baha'i International Community was granted consultative status with the Economic and Social Council (ECOSOC), and in 1976 with the United Nations Children's

Fund (UNICEF). It has representatives at United Nations in New York and Geneva, and with the Environment Programme in Nairobi.

Teachings of the Baha'i Faith

Some basic Baha'i Principles proclaimed by Baha'u'llah for this age:

- The oneness of mankind.
- Independent investigation of truth.
- The common foundation of all religions.
- The essential harmony of science and religion.
- Equality of men and women.
- Elimination of prejudice of all kinds.
- Universal compulsory education.
- A spiritual solution of the economic problem.
- A universal auxiliary language.
- Universal peace.

Loyalty to Government

The Baha'i Writings state clearly that it is the unquestioned duty of the Baha'is in every land *"to demonstrate their unqualified loyalty and obedience to whatever is the considered judgment of their respective governments."*

According to the direct and sacred command of Baha'u'llah the Baha'is are forbidden to utter slander, are commanded to show forth peace and amity, are exhorted to rectitude of conduct, straight-fowardness and harmony with all the kindreds and people of the world. They must obey and be the well-wishers of the government of the land.

Obedience to a duly constituted government means submission to all of its laws and regulations, the only exception being when a government demands actions which amount to a repudiation of the Faith.

Baha'is are specifically forbidden by Baha'u'llah to take part in any subversive political, social or anti-religious movements, nor can they be members of political parties or secret organisations.

"We Baha'is are one the world over; we are seeking to build up a new World Order, divine in origin. How can we do this if

every Baha'i is a member of a different political party — some of them diametrically opposite to each other? Where is our unity then? We would be divided, because of politics, against ourselves, and this is the opposite of our purpose.

Shoghi Effendi

It is the cherished desire of every true follower of Baha'u'llah to serve the interests of his country in an unselfish and truly patriotic way, whilst at the same time not deviating from upholding the high standards enshrined in the Teachings of the Baha'i Faith.

Social Laws of the Baha'i Faith

Marriage

Monogamous marriage is encouraged by Baha'u'llah.

"Marry, O people, that from you may appear he who will remember Me amongst My servants; this is one of My commandments unto you. Obey it as an assistance to yourselves."

Baha'u'llah

He has made marriage conditional upon the consent of both parties and of their parents.

"As We desired to bring about love and friendship and the unity of the people, therefore We made it (marriage) conditional upon the consent of the parents also, that enmity and ill-feeling might be avoided."

Baha'u'llah

Divorce

Divorce is permitted in the Baha'i Faith, but strongly discouraged.

"The Friends (Baha'is) must strictly refrain from divorce unless something arises which compels them to separate because of their aversion from each other; ... They must then be patient and wait one complete year. If during this year harmony is not re-established between them, then divorce may be realised ..."

'Abdu'l-Baha

Prayer and Fasting

Baha'u'llah and 'Abdu'l-Baha have revealed innumerable prayers for the use of their followers at various times and for various purposes.

Fasting, together with the obligatory prayers, constitutes

the two pillars that sustain the revealed Word of God. Baha'is fast from sunrise to sunset for nineteen days every year, from March 2 to 21.

Some Prohibitions

The following are not permitted to Baha'is — intoxicating drinks, opium and other habit-forming drugs, gambling, theft, violence, striking or wounding a person, adultery, homosexuality, back-biting and calumny.

Purpose of Religion

"The fundamental purpose animating the Faith of God and His Religion is to safeguard the interests and promote the unity of the human race, and to foster the spirit of love and fellowship amongst men." Baha'u'llah

". . . religion must be the cause of unity, harmony and agreement among mankind. If it be the cause of discord and hostility, if it leads to separation and creates conflict, the absence of religion would be preferable in the world."

'Abdu'l-Baha

Oneness of Mankind

"Ye are the fruits of one tree and the leaves of one branch." Baha'u'llah

"Let there be no mistake. The principle of the oneness of mankind — the pivot round which all the teachings of Baha'u'llah revolve is no mere outburst of ignorant emotionalism or an expression of vague and pious hope. Its appeal is not to be merely identified with a reawakening of the spirit of brotherhood and goodwill among men, nor does it aim solely at the fostering of harmonious co-operation among individual peoples and nations. Its implications are deeper, its claims greater than any which the Prophets of old were allowed to advance. Its message is applicable not only to the individual, but concerns itself primarily with the nature of those essential relationships that must bind all the states and nations as members of one human family. It calls for no less than the reconstruction and the demilitarisation of the whole civilised world — a world organically unified in all the essen-

tial aspects of its life, its political machinery, its spiritual aspiration, its trade and finance, its script and language, and yet infinite in the diversity of the national characteristics of its federated units.

"It represents the consummation of human evolution, an evolution that has had its earliest beginnings in the birth of family life, its subsequent development in the achievement of tribal solidarity, leading in turn to the constitution of the city-state, and expanding later into the institution of independent and sovereign nations.

"The principle of the oneness of mankind, as proclaimed by Baha'u'llah, carries with it no more and no less than a solemn assertion that its realisation is fast approaching, and that nothing short of a power born of God can succeed in establishing it."   Shoghi Effendi

Oneness of Religion

"The gift of God to the enlightened age is the knowledge of the oneness of mankind and the fundamental oneness of religion."   'Abdu'l-Baha

Baha'is believe that all the great religions of the world are divine in origin. They have all been revealed by God in different places and different ages according to the evolving needs and capacities of the people. No age has been without guidance from God and as long as there are men on earth, God will give them guidance.

God Himself is above and beyond human understanding. His guidance is given to men through His Messengers, perfect and stainless souls who are referred to as Manifestations of God. These Manifestations of God are not God themselves but they are like perfect mirrors reflecting the light of God to men. They are like the rays of the sun to earth, which transmit the light of the sun to earth, they are the intermediaries between God and humanity. They reflect in their lives and teachings the perfections of God. Through these Manifestations, God causes man to know and love Him. Knowledge of God is only possible for man through these Manifestations, and knowledge of their perfections is the fullest knowledge of God to which finite minds can attain.

The appearance of a Manifestation of God on earth is a rare event. History records the names of but a few: Krishna, Abraham, Zoroaster, Moses, Buddha, Jesus, Muhammad, the Bab and Baha'u'llah. Each one of Them has founded a religion and inspired a civilisation. Each one was bitterly opposed, ridiculed, scorned and ill-treated by the people amongst whom They first appeared. Only a few of Their contemporaries recognised Their station. Gradually, other men grew to recognise Them. After Their lives on earth were over, They were and still are loved, revered and followed by millions. Alone and unaided by earthly power, They established Their sovereignty over the hearts of men. They are the true Educators of humanity Whose purpose is to draw men ever nearer to God and to assist in the advancement of human civilisation.

Abolition of Prejudices

A new religious principles is that prejudice and fanaticism whether sectarian, denominational, patriotic or political are destructive to the foundation of human solidarity; therefore man should release himself from such bonds in order that the oneness of the world of humanity may become manifest. *"Light is good in whatever lamp it is burning".*
"A rose is beautiful in whatsoever garden it may bloom."
"A star has the same radiance whether it shines from the East or the West."   'Abdu'l-Baha

Justice is a paramount teaching of the Faith. Baha'is are commanded to deal justly with all people.

CENTRAL FIGURES OF THE BAHA'I FAITH

The Bab

Siyyid 'Ali Muhammad, known by the title Bab (translated 'Gate' or 'Door'), proclaimed in 1844, in the Persian city of Shiraz, that a new day had dawned; that the promises of all religions relating to an era of peace and brotherhood — in fact the Kingdom of God on earth — was about to be inaugurated by the Great Prophet, the Promised One of all ages.

The Bab, whilst claiming Himself to be a Prophet of God, taught that the purpose of His Mission was to prepare the way for, and herald the appearance of the Promised One.

As a result of His claims and teachings the Bab and His followers were subjected to the hatred of fanatical religious orthodoxy and were persecuted by both religious and governmental forces. The Bab was finally executed in Tabriz in 1850. In those first few years over 20,000 of the Bab's followers were brutally murdered.

Some 50 years later the remains of the Bab were eventually transferred to their resting place in the Shrine of the Bab on Mount Carmel in Haifa, Israel.

Baha'u'llah

Mirza Husayn 'Ali, known as Baha'u'llah (translated: 'The Glory of God') was the son of a Minister in the Court of the Shah. From an early age He was distinguished from others by His extraordinary wisdom, intelligence and knowledge. Although He received no formal schooling He was capable of solving the most difficult problems, and in whatever meeting He was found He became the authority of explanation upon intricate and abstruse questions.

As soon as He was informed of the teachings of the Bab He declared them to be true. Because He espoused the Cause of the Bab He suffered torture, imprisonment and banishment from Persia, first to Baghdad (1853), then to Constantinople and Adrianople (1863) and finally to 'Akka, Palestine (1868).

It was in Baghdad in 1863 that Baha'u'llah proclaimed that He was the One foretold by the Bab, the Promised One of all religions. In 1868 He began His public proclamation, addressed primarily to the rulers of the world, individually and collectively, including Queen Victoria, Napoleon III, Czar Alexander II, Kaiser Wilhelm I, Emperor Francis Joseph, Sultan 'Abdul'l-Aziz, Nasirir'd-Din Shah and Pope Pius IX. It was in 'Akka that He revealed His Book of Laws. Throughout His exile He revealed thousands of verses which make up the one hundred or more volumes of His works and which, together with the Writings of the Bab and of 'Abdu'l-Baha, form the extensive Baha'i Scriptures.

Baha'u'llah's earthly life ended in 1892 and His remains were laid to rest at Bahji on the outskirts of 'Akka, facing Mount Carmel across the Bay of Haifa.

'Abdu'l-Baha

Abbas Effendi, known as 'Abdu'l-Baha (translated: 'Servant of Baha', or 'Servant of the Glory') was Baha'u'llah's eldest son. He accompanied His Father throughout all His exiles, beginning in 1853 at the age of nine, and only regained His freedom in 1908 when the Young Turk Revolution freed prisoners of the Ottoman Empire. Baha'u'llah, in His Will and Testament, indicated that on His passing the Baha'is should turn to 'Abdul'l-Baha as the Centre of His Covenant and Head of the Faith.

In 1898, whilst still a prisoner, 'Abdu'l-Baha was visited in 'Akka by the first group of pilgrims from the West who came to investigate the new Faith. And so, at the end of the 19th century the Baha'i Faith spread to the United States, Canada, Britain and Europe.

'Abdu'l-Baha visited Europe, Britain, the United States and Canada during 1911 and 1912, further spreading the new Faith in those countries. In 1920, 'Abdu'l-Baha was invested with the insignia of the Knighthood of the British Empire, conferred upon Him in recognition of His humanitarian work in Palestine during the war for the relief of distress and famine. He accepted the honour as the gift of a 'just king' but never used the title. He died in Haifa in 1921 and was buried on Mount Carmel in the same shrine as the Bab.

In His Will and Testament, 'Abdu'l-Baha appointed His grandson Shoghi Effendi as Guardian of the Faith, the Head to whom all Baha'is should turn, thus protecting the infant Faith from schism.

Shoghi Effendi

Under the direction of Shoghi Effendi, the Guardian of the Baha'i Faith, the Faith spread rapdily, reaching right across the world by the time of his passing in November 1957 at the age of 60. During his thirty-six year ministry in almost

15,000 authenticated letters written mostly in superb English, but also in Arabic and Persian, Shoghi Effendi developed the loosely-knit body of believers living in some thirty-five countries at the time of 'Abdu'l-Baha's passing into a world-wide unified and progressive community dedicated to a global crusade in two hundred countries. This work carried on after his death and in 1963 the supreme administrative governing body of the Baha'i Faith, the Universal House of Justice, ordained and described in detail in Baha'i Scripture, was elected by delegates from fifty-six national administrative bodies.

BAHA'I ADMINISTRATION

Unlike the Founders of earlier world religions, Baha'u'llah made specific provision for an administrative system as an integral part of His Revelation.

The affairs of the Baha'i Faith throughout the world are administered by elected bodies on international, national and local levels. Electioneering and nomination are not permitted, the elector choosing only *". . . those whom prayer and reflection have inspired him to uphold . . . to consider without the least trace of passion and prejudice, and irrespective of any material consideration, the names of only those who can best combine the necessary qualities of unquestioned loyalty, of selfless devotion, of a well-trained mind, of recognised ability and mature experience."*

Shoghi Effendi

The Universal House of Justice

Elected every five years by delegates from all national Baha'i communities, this international governing body functions from its seat in Haifa, Israel, the World Centre of the Faith. The Holy Land is the spritual centre of the Baha'i Faith by reason of its three Central Figures being buried there, and at the command of Baha'u'llah it is also the centre of its world-embracing Administration. The Universal House of Justice directs the progress of the Faith and the application of the teachings of Baha'u'llah to an evolving world community. The Universal House of Justice is invested with authority to enact laws not specifically revealed by Baha'u'llah, to meet the needs of the evolving society.

National Spiritual Assemblies

These nine-member bodies are responsible for the administration of the affairs of the Baha'i Faith on a national level in the area they represent. Elected each year by delegates representing the Baha'is throughout the geographical region, the role of each National Spiritual Assembly is to stimulate, unify and co-ordinate the activites of the Baha'is and direct the general affairs of the Faith throughout the land.

Local Spiritual Assemblies

These bodies which operate at the local level are also comprised of nine, annually elected, members. Each year the members of every local community which has nine or more adult members choose, by the same prayerful election process, those whom they believe to be most suited to adminster the affairs of the community.

* * *

At all levels of Baha'i Administration decision-making is by the process of Baha'i consultation, where each member of the elected body has equal rights and obligations of self-expression, where the clash of differing opinions is welcomed but the clash of personalities is not permitted. When decision has been reached, either by unanimous agreement or majority vote, all members work for its implementation, any minority dissention being subordinated to the will of the majority.

APPENDIX TWO

Correspondence about the Situation of the Baha'is in Iran

Letter from Lord McNair to The Times, *Monday 27 July 1981*

Sir, On July 16 you raised your powerful voice in protest against the ruling Iranian clergy's executions of their opponents. No one could dissent, though some may wonder how benignly the Mujahiddin-e-Khalq would treat *their* opponents if they were on top.

Will you, I beg, also use your influence to mobilise world opinion against the persecution of the harmless, non-political followers of the Baha'i faith, a persecution which has continued under almost all the regimes which have followed each other in Iran for the past 140 years and which is plumbing new depths of savagery under this one?

This barbarism now threatens to reach the level of mass-martyrdom. I use that work in its most literal sense. Of the 62 Baha'is judicially executed since the last revolution many were offered their lives in exchange for the abandonment of their religious beliefs. All refused. The number who have lost their lives at the hands of mullah-led lynch mobs is harder to ascertain.

In addition to the killings and beatings this exercise in scapegoat-politics takes all the sickeningly usual forms, systematic destruction of the community's economic base, denial of education and employment, desecration of holy shrines and of cemeteries.

Your readers may ask, Sir, what is this faith for which men choose to die and which is so repugnant to the followers of the Ayatollah, who denies it even the small measure of recognition he grants to Christianity, Judaism and Zoroastrianism. Arising out of nineteenth-century Islam, the Baha'i faith asserts the essential oneness of God and of all the great revealed religions, Judaism, Christianity, Islam and Buddhism.

On the ethical side they take no part in politics, giving allegiance to whatever secular power they happen to live under. (In this they resemble the more fortunate Druses in the Middle East. In Christian language they "render unto Caesar ...") They attach great importance to education, especially that of women. They hold the most enlightened views about what we call industrial relations, believing that the worker should share responsibility for the direction of his enterprise with his employer. They aspire to a world authority instead of our present chaotic patchwork of nationalisms. No wonder that Professor Gilbert Murray described them as "the peaceful followers of a harmless and progressive religion", but that was at the time of the 1955 wave of persecution under the Shah's regime.

How then should we respond to the persecution of these people? Certainly not, I suggest, by condemning Islam as such. There must surely be better, saner elements even in the Islamic Revolutionary Party who know that all these acts of barbarism disgrace Islam and can do nothing but damage to Iran. How can we reach them? It is terribly urgent that we do.

Yours,
JOHN McNAIR
House of Lords,
July 21

Letter to Dr. Kurt Waldheim, United Nations, New York, from thirteen heads of Oxford University Colleges, June 1981.

Headed: Trinity College, Oxford.

Dear Dr Waldheim,

We are horrified by the recent persecution in Iran of members of the Baha'i Faith and other minorities.

We note the scale and severity of persecution have greatly increased in recent weeks.

The European Parliament has passed resolutions in September 1980 and April 1981 condemning such persecution.

Since then the situation has become much more serious.

We urge international public opinion to do all it can to persuade the Government of Iran to cease the persecution of these law-abiding, religious people, who are in no way involved in political matters.

signed

Sir Geoffrey G. Arthur: Master, Pembroke

Dr Arthur H. Cooke: Warden, New College

Mr Raymond M. Carr: Warden, St Anthony's

Dr Gerald E. Aylmer: Master, St Peter's

Dr Keith B. Griffin: President, Magdalen

The Honourable Sir Henry A.P. Fisher, Q.C. President, Wolfson

Sir Stuart Hampshire: Warden, Wadham

Mr Anthony Quinton: President, Trinity

The Right Honourable Lord Asa Briggs: Provost, Worcester

The Right Honourable Lord Robert Blake: Provost, Queens

Sir John Habakkuk: Principal, Jesus

Mr Geoffrey J. Warnock: Principal, Hertford — and The Vice-Chancellor elect

Mr Michael G. Brock: Warden, Nuffield

Letter from the Dean of Westminster to Mr Stanley Clinton Davis, M.P., 8 July 1981

Dear Mr Clinton Davis,
My heart goes out in sympathy to the Bahais who are living in Iran at this time and as a consequence are undergoing relentless persecution though they are peace-loving and of high integrity.
I hope that this meeting,* which nothing but a prior engagement which I could not get out of, would have prevented my attending, every success and I hope that from it there will come a strong request to Her Majesty's Government to use the maximum diplomatic pressure upon the authorities in Iran to bring relief to the Bahais from their intolerable situation.

Yours sincerely,
Edward Carpenter

Cable from U.K. Baha'is to Iranian Leaders Following Completion of Demolition of House of the Bab in Shiraz, November 1979

MR ABOL HASSAN BANISADR, ACTING FOREIGN MINISTER, TEHRAN
AYATOLLAH BEHESHTI, SECRETARY, REVOLUTIONARY COUNCIL, TEHRAN

BRITISH BAHA'I COMMUNITY DISMAYED NEWS RENEWED ATTACK ON HOUSE OF THE BAB 9 NOVEMBER RAZING GROUND THIS HOLY SHRINE. THIS ODIOUS ACT PERPETRATED DESPITE ASSURANCES THAT GOVERNMENT ISLAMIC REPUBLIC HAD NO INTENTION DESTROYING BAHA'I SHRINES. APPEAL YOUR EXCELLENCY'S PREVENTION FURTHER DAMAGE HOLY HOUSE AND ITS PRECINCTS. RESPECTFULLY APPEAL IRANIAN AUTHORITIES HONOUR TRUE ISLAMIC TOLERANCE RETURN TO BAHA'I COMMUNITY ALL PROPER-

* see page 123

TIES HELD SACRED BY BAHAI'S IN UNITED KINGDOM AND WORLD OVER. BESEECH YOUR EXCELLENCY TO EXERCISE JUSTICE AND GOODWILL IN THIS AFFAIR.

NATIONAL SPIRITUAL ASSEMBLY BAHA'IS UNITED KINGDOM BAHA'I LONDON SW7

Cable Sent by U.K. Baha'is to President and Prime Minister of Iran after Execution of Baha'is in Yazd, 9 September 1980

WITH DEEP SHOCK RELATE YOUR EXCELLENCY HEART RENDING NEWS CRUEL EXECUTION MONDAY 9 SEPTEMBER SEVEN INNOCENT BAHA'IS IN YAZD. LOCAL REVOLUTIONARY GUARDS WHO PERPETRATED THIS COWARDLY ACT FALSELY ACCUSED THESE INNOCENT BAHA'IS OF SPYING AND SUB-VERSIVE ACTIVITIES. APPEAL YOUR EXCELLENCY PREVENT SUCH IRRESPONSIBLE ACTS SUCH MALICIOUS FALSE ACCU-SATIONS BY FANATICAL SCHEMING ELEMENTS AGAINST MEMBERS LAW-ABIDING BAHA'I COMMUNITY. BAHA'IS IN IRAN AND ELSEWHERE HAVE REPEATEDLY ANNOUNCED AND WILL CONTINUE TO PROCLAIM THEIR FUNDAMENTAL RELIGIOUS BELIEF IN OBEDIENCE TO THEIR GOVERNMENT AND NON-INVOLVEMENT IN POLITICAL AND SUBVERSIVE ACTIVITIES. APPEAL YOUR EXCELLENCY PROTECT FAIR NAME ISLAM AND HONOUR BELOVED LAND IRAN FROM SHAMELESS ACTS SCHEMING ELEMENTS.

NATIONAL SPIRITUAL ASSEMBLY BAHA'IS UNITED KING-DOM

International Declaration Regarding the Baha'is

UNANIMOUS RESOLUTION PASSED BY THE EUROPEAN PARLIAMENT IN STRASBOURG, ON FRIDAY, 19 SEPTEMBER 1980, CONCERNING THE RIGHTS OF THE BAHA'I COMMUNITY IN IRAN

The European Parliament

— recalling its unfailing attachment to international protection of human rights.

— recognizing in particular the need to protect the rights of religious minorities in all countries.

— concerned at the systematic campaign of persecution directed in Iran against the 300,000 members of the Baha'i community (the biggest religious minority in Iran) and the accompanying violations of elementary human rights, in particular:

(a) the refusal of any legal protection to the Baha'i minority,

(b) the summary arrest, detention and execution of leaders of the Baha'i community,

(c) the confiscation or destruction of the resources and means of subsistence of the Baha'i and the arbitrary dismissals or refusals to employ Baha'is,

(d) the threats and acts of violence against the Baha'is in an attempt to force them to repudiate their Faith,

    i) condemns the violation of the human rights of all religious minorities in Iran, more particularly the members of the Baha'i Faith, whose rights as a religious minority are not recognised by the Iranian Constitution;

ii) calls upon the Government of Iran to grant the Baha'i community the legal recognition and protection to which all minorities are entitled under the provisions of the various UN Acts and Conventions on human rights;

iii) also condemns the illegal measures taken against Catholic and Anglican leaders, and the execution of leading members of the Jewish community;

iv) calls upon the Foreign Ministers of the European Communities meeting in political cooperation to make urgent representations to the Iranian authorities to put an end to the persecution of the members of the Baha'i community, and to allow them to practise their religion freely and enjoy all civil, political, social, economic and cultural rights, requests the Commission and Council of the European Communities to impose an embargo on all sales of surplus agricultural products to Iran where subsidies by European taxpayers are involved until full human rights are restored to Iranian citizens;

v) instructs its President to forward this Resolution to the Foreign Ministers meeting in political cooperation, to the Government of Iran, to the Governments and Parliaments of the Member States and to the Secretary General of the United Nations.

Justification

All the evidence suggests that the arrests and executions of the Baha'is are continuing to increase and are being carried out according to a pre-arranged plan. Only a speedy response by the European Parliament can stop these developments.

BIBLIOGRAPHICAL NOTE

Interest in Iranian history has grown as a result of the recent Islamic Revolution. The most enlightening work on Shi'ih ideology and its shaping influence on the revolution is M.M.J. Fisher's: *Iran From Religious Dispute to Revolution.* Harvard University Press, 1980. Political and economic analyses of Pahlavi Iran are easy to come by; an interesting, if partisan account of the Shah's rule and the events that overthrew him, is Fereydoun Hoveyda's: *The Fall of the Shah*, translated from the French and published by Weidenfeld and Nicolson, 1980.

There is unfortunately a dearth of scholarly, unbiased literature on the Babi and Baha'i religions. Among the Baha'i sources there is Shoghi Effendi's history of the first one hundred years of the Babi-Baha'i movement, the literary masterpiece, *God Passes By*, Baha'i Publishing Trust, Wilmette, 1970. Much primary material is to be found in the works of the historian of the Baha'i Faith and Islam, H.M. Balyuzi, who has written a trilogy on the three central figures of the new religion. A reasonable text book on Baha'i belief is John Ferraby's: *All Things Made New*, Baha'i Publishing Trust, Oakham, 1975. A long-standing opponent of the Baha'is, the missionary, William Miller, has written several books on the religion, of doubtful historical and scholarly veracity.

Classic nineteenth century accounts of the Babi-Baha'i religions by Gobineau, Nicholas, E.G. Browne, and Lord Curzon are still well worth consulting; the reader should first acquire Moojan Momen's *The Babi and Baha'i Religions 1844–1944*, George Ronald, Oxford, 1981. This work is subtitled: 'Some contemporary Western Accounts' and provides a detailed bibliography and notes for students of non-Baha'i accounts of the first century of the Baha'i Faith. I acknowledge my debt to this work for the documentary material I have quoted in the present volume. My own forthcoming publication, *The Phoenix and the Ashes*, George Ronald, Oxford, discusses Baha'i attitudes to modern history and the continuing crisis of contemporary society.